# Collins

## Student Support Materials for

## OCR A2 Sociology

# Unit G674

## Social Inequality and Difference with Research Methods

Authors: Viv Thompson and
Fionnuala Swann
Series editor: Peter Langley

Published by Collins Education

An imprint of HarperCollins Publishers

77-85 Fulham Palace Road

Hammersmith

London

W6 8JB

Browse the complete Collins Education catalogue at
**www.collinseducation.com**

ISBN 978-0-00-741838-1

Fionnuala Swann and Viv Thompson assert their moral rights to be identified as the authors of this work.

British Library Cataloguing in Publication Data.

A catalogue record for this publication is available from the British Library.

Commissioned by Charlie Evans and Andrew Campbell

Project editor: Sarah Vittachi

Design and typesetting by Hedgehog Publishing Limited

Cover Design by Angela English

Production by Simon Moore

Printed and bound by L.E.G.O. S.p.A. Italy

Indexed by Indexing Specialists (UK) Ltd

Acknowledgements

Every effort has been made to contact the holders of copyright material, but if any have been inadvertently overlooked the publishers will be pleased to make the necessary arrangements at the first opportunity.

p5, Table 1, source: *The Hills Report* (2010), Government Equalities Office; p6, Key study, source: Higher Education Statistics Agency; p8, fig 1, source: ONS 2009; p14, Key study, source: K Bhopal, 'South Asian Women Homeworkers in East London' in Gregory et al. *Women, Work and Inequality* (1999), Macmillan; p16, source: ONS 2010; p17, Key study, source: J Midgely and R Bradshaw, 'Should I Stay or Should I Go?' *Rural Youth Transitions* (2006), IPPR and CRC; p31, Key study, source: H S Mirza, *Young, Female and Black* (1992), Routledge; p36, Key study, source: M Hollingsworth and S Lansley, *From Russia with Cash: The Inside Story of the Oligarchs* (2010), HarperCollins; p38, Key Study, source: F Devine, *Class Practices: How Parents Help Their Children Get Good Jobs* (2004), Cambridge University Press; p52, Key Study, source: H Hauari and K Hollingworth, *Understanding Fathering: Masculinity, Diversity and Change* (2009), Joseph Rowntree Foundation; p67, Key study, source: S Blackman, 'Destructing a Giro: A Critical and Ethnographic Study of the Youth 'Underclass'', R MacDonald (ed.) *Youth, the 'Underclass' and Social Exclusion* (1997) Routledge; p69, source: H Becker, Whose Side Are We On? *Social Problems*, 14, (1967), 239–47, University of California Press; p82, source: C Griffin et al. 'Every Time I Do It I Absolutely Annihilate Myself': Loss of (Self) Consciousness and Loss of Memory in Young People's Drinking Narratives, *Sociology (*2009) 43: 457, Routledge; p90, source: S Ball and C Vincent, ''Making up' the middle-class child: Families, activities and class dispositions', *Sociology* 41: 1061 (2007), Routledge.

Thanks to the following students for providing answers to the questions:

Ruby Barwood, Collette Blackman, Lauren Foley, Vicki Gill, Jessica Gowers, Fran Guratsky, Rachel Hewitt, Ella Keating, Charlotte Ross, Eric Wedge-Bull.

# Contents

## What is social inequality and difference?

**Social differences** may be based on material factors such as wealth and income, and cultural factors such as ethnicity; these differences may lead to **social inequalities**. Social differences might be based on gender, age, religion, sexual orientation or class, and social inequalities might occur as a result of these differences. However, social differences do not necessarily lead to social inequalities. MacDonald and Marsh (2005) found that when young men and women experienced unemployment, the gender difference was not a factor, whereas gender difference is a factor for many women in employment who, on average, earn less than men (the **gender pay gap**) or find they are not able to gain promotion as easily as men (**vertical segregation**).

### Essential notes

Some social groups, such as single parents, the disabled, the long-term unemployed and some minority ethnic groups, are more vulnerable to poverty than others. You should know some of the reasons for this, such as lack of educational qualifications, expensive childcare, rising unemployment and **discrimination**.

### Essential notes

Life chances means the extent to which individuals and households are able to access resources seen as desirable in society, such as health care, housing, education and employment. These are affected by social differences; for example, when unemployment is rising, the competition for jobs increases and some groups are more likely to be excluded from the labour market. This leads to social inequalities.

### Key study

MacDonald and Marsh carried out in-depth research, using **semi-structured interviews** and **observation**, on young working-class people in Teesside. They found that, whilst there was a very high unemployment rate in the area compared to more affluent areas in the UK, the study group shared the dominant values of mainstream society. They did not deliberately choose to be unemployed and live on the dole.

"Getting a job is the main object, isn't it? … Without a job, you're stuck. Nowhere to go. You're stuck in a dead end, aren't you?" (Leo, 18)

"I would like to live with my boyfriend, but not until we've both got jobs and … can … afford it." (Elizabeth, 19)

### Social inequalities

Social inequalities are based on the extent to which individuals or groups have more or less power, status, wealth and income. These are unequally distributed in society; for example:

- gender – women often experience inequalities in relation to lower employment status and less pay
- ethnicity – some minority ethnic groups experience inequalities in relation to employment and consequently to pay/income and status
- age – the young and old often experience inequalities in relation to status and power in terms of how they are treated in society; for example, seen as 'vulnerable' and to be 'looked after'
- class – linked to social, economic and cultural capital; social classes 1, 2 and 3 of the National Statistics Socio-economic Classification have greater status, wealth and income than 4, 5, 6 and 7.

Social inequalities can lead to **poverty**, which may then lead to further inequalities linked to a decrease in an individual's **life chances**. Payne (2006) argues some groups have more power than others, which gives them a social advantage. This is then related to their unequal share of material resources. Social inequality is also important; if people have less power, status and wealth than others they may not be able to fully participate in society, and may feel excluded from those things the majority take for granted.

### Inequality – ups and downs

The Institute for Fiscal Studies (2009) found that, whilst inequality rose very steeply in the period 1979–1991, it has been up and down in the last 20 years. The Hills Report (2010) points out that the richest 1% of the population are now receiving more of the total income available in the UK than they were in the 1970s. However, as the table below shows, inequality is more than just considering the richest and poorest. Ethnicity is also an important factor. **Table 1** divides the British population into fifths (quintiles) according to their income. The bottom quintile are the fifth with the lowest incomes, and the top quintile are the fifth with the highest.

| Percentage of individuals | Bottom quintile | Second quintile | Middle quintile | Fourth quintile | Top quintile |
|---|---|---|---|---|---|
| White | 18 | 20 | 20 | 21 | 21 |
| Indian | 27 | 18 | 20 | 14 | 21 |
| Pakistani and Bangladeshi | 54 | 27 | 9 | 6 | 4 |
| African-Caribbean | 30 | 22 | 18 | 16 | 13 |
| Chinese | 34 | 16 | 18 | 16 | 16 |

**Table 1**
Quintile distribution of income for individuals by ethnicity (2008/9)

### Social mobility

Education has been seen as a route for the working class to move into the middle class.

The Higher Education Funding Council for England (2010) points out that the numbers of poorer children entering higher education rose between 1994 and 2009. Evidence from the Organization for Economic Cooperation and Development (2010) demonstrates that there is a strong correlation between fathers who have degrees and the wage level of their children.

The increased number of working-class children entering higher education led to some social upward mobility between 1994 and 2009. Williams (2010) suggests that these working-class children may pass on this advantage to their own children, reinforcing the social mobility they have experienced themselves. However, the numbers of working-class students entering higher education may change as fees rise. Poorer children and their parents may be reluctant to pay the high fees, given the uncertainty of the labour market and postgraduate employment rates.

### Examiners' notes

Impress examiners by keeping up to date with statistics illustrating social inequalities, such as rates of employment by ethnic group or working-class access to top universities, by using websites such as www.ons.gov.uk or www.hesa.ac.uk. However, always consider the extent to which the sources of the data can be trusted.

### Examiners' notes

Make sure you know other examples of social inequalities and differences from the units you have already studied. Ensure you can identify empirical research that supports your chosen examples; for example, Archer's (2003) research on Muslim boys is an example of social inequalities that may occur as a result of differences in gender as well as class and race.

## Measuring social class

Measuring **social class** is challenging. Sociologists have competing views as to how to determine who should be where in the class structure. Marxists argue that the ownership of the means of production determines class position, while Weberians argue that power and status must also be taken into account. At a descriptive rather than theoretical level, social class could be based on factors such as income, education, wealth, lifestyle, status or occupation.

### Group interests

A number of groups have an interest in using a consistent measure.

Sociologists – it means they can compare research findings and make claims regarding the **validity/reliability** of those findings or identify **patterns** and **trends**. The data collected by HESA (see below) is useful for sociologists when examining class inequalities.

Governments – who want to develop social policies on, for example, the numbers of working-class students entering university.

Advertisers and industry – who want to identify areas where they should target goods and services. Sales of luxury goods are likely to be higher in areas dominated by the highest social classes.

The government has set targets for the numbers of students entering university from disadvantaged backgrounds. Data collected by HESA in the study below enables them to check the extent to which they are meeting their targets.

### Key study

Research by HESA (Higher Education Statistics Agency) on the percentage of students attending universities from routine/manual occupational backgrounds in 2008/9 found the following data:

| Subject | % of students |
| --- | --- |
| Medicine, dentistry and veterinary | 18.3 |
| History and philosophical studies | 24.2 |
| Engineering and technology | 31.1 |
| Social studies | 31.1 |
| Computer sciences | 38.9 |
| Education | 41.4 |

The data also showed 12.8% of students at Cambridge were from routine or manual occupational backgrounds 11.5% at Oxford, and 21.9% at Newcastle, whereas the percentage at Bolton was 52.3%, Bradford 52.4% and Greenwich 55.5%.

### The Registrar General classification scheme

In 1911 the Registrar General (RG) devised a classification scheme based on occupation, which was used until 2000. The RG scale provided a useful means of differentiating between the working class and middle class.

It was used by governments when devising **social policies,** particularly those relating to health and education; and provided sociologists with a consistent measure to use as a basis for their research.

Occupation often indicates who a person or household mixes with. It is the shared experiences, identity and status accompanying occupation that makes it such a useful measure of social class. It can indicate educational qualifications, income, lifestyle and cultural capital.

The RG scale omitted:

- the unemployed and never-employed
- women who did not have a paid job outside the home
- single mothers who worked
- the very wealthy who lived off the income from their wealth.

In addition:

- it grouped occupations together without differentiating between lifestyles of people from different occupations in the same class
- it was based on the assumption that the head of household was male even if a woman was the main wage earner
- it took no account of rising unemployment
- it took no account of the increasing participation of women in the labour market
- it largely ignored the self-employed.

### The National Statistics Socio-economic Classification (NS-SEC)

In the census of 2001 a new occupational scheme (the NS-SEC), developed by Weberian sociologists, was used. It took account of:

- status and power as well as occupation
- pay, hours, education, housing, income and occupational level.

The NS-SEC dealt with some of the issues raised by feminists. The head of household is based on the highest income earner, and if it is a dual income household and incomes are equal then age is taken as the means to identify the head of household.

### Evaluation of the NS-SEC

- It is still based on occupation and does not take account of the very wealthy, nor those who do not work. However, it does include those who are unemployed and want to work.
- It is based partly on educational qualifications, but skilled trades operatives tend to be higher paid than administrative and secretarial staff, although the latter are placed in a higher social class because they tend to have higher educational qualifications.
- It does not take account of how class is lived. People are grouped together who do not share the same lifestyle.
- It does not take account of how people see themselves – when asked about their social class, people often take factors such as education and housing into account.

### Essential notes

There are some sociologists who were unhappy with the RG scale; for example feminists, notably Arber, Dale and Gilbert (1986), who developed a 'feminist alternative' known as the Surrey Occupational Class Schema, and Weberians such as Hope and Goldthorpe who developed and used an alternative classification.

### Examiners' notes

Ensure you know why the change from the RG scale to the NS-SEC was made and that you understand the differences between them, as well as the different problems each raises.

## Essential notes

Official statistics are quantitative data produced by the government. They are based on surveys, from the census, which covers all households in the UK, to large-scale national sample surveys plus some smaller-scale local surveys. Much of the data collected is published via Social Trends or the Office for National Statistics (ONS).

## Social class and inequality: income, wealth and housing

### Income and wealth

There is a clear link between income and wealth and inequality. The evidence for this comes partly from large-scale national surveys carried out by the government such as the Labour Force Survey, the Family Resources Survey and the Living Costs and Food Survey. These surveys provide a considerable amount of information, but none are comprehensive.

The data below on household income is from the Office for National Statistics. However, it is difficult to include household income of all social groups. Access to some groups may be difficult; for example, travellers, the homeless, or the very wealthy with households overseas as well as in the UK. The extent to which the official statistics derived from these surveys can provide a valid picture is uncertain.

**Fig 1**
UK – original income and final income 2008/9

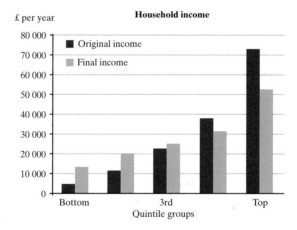

The blue columns in the bar chart identify household income of the UK population before taxes and benefits. The green columns depict household income after taxes and benefits were added. The addition of benefits reduces the inequality gap but the differential between the bottom fifth and the top fifth is still approximately £40 000.

### Household income

Apart from access to those not living in households, there are a number of other issues with regard to household income statistics.

## Essential notes

Benefits include pension credits, income support, incapacity benefit and pensions. It is important to distinguish between income and wealth. Taking wealth into account significantly increases the difference between rich and poor.

## Examiners' notes

A brief evaluative comment on the method used by the research evidence (in this case official statistics, which for the sociologist is secondary data) will demonstrate to the examiner that you are using evidence in a critical way.

- There are a number of ways of measuring income. Two of the ways are used in the ONS bar chart, before and after benefits.
- **Operationalizing** income can differ from one survey to another.
- Some social groups, such as the very wealthy or those who work for 'cash-in-hand', may be omitted from some records.
- A sample may not be representative of all social groups where, for example, a group is comparatively small.

- Some self-employed people are not VAT-registered and therefore do not appear in the records of HM Revenue and Customs.
- Bonuses are sometimes paid in kind or in other ways that exclude those who receive them from full taxation.
- Some people live in off-shore tax havens.

Since 1979 the gap between the rich and poor has increased. During the Conservative governments of 1979–1997 it widened significantly (New Earnings Survey 2008). This gap stabilized under the Labour governments of 1997–2010 but did not decrease.

The Institute for Fiscal Studies (2007) argues that income inequality is now greater than at the end of the Second World War. The UK has the eighth worst level of inequality compared to other EU countries (Social Trends, 2010)). Save the Children (2009) found that 13% of children in the UK were living in severe poverty. The Hills Report (2010), funded by the government, and by far the most comprehensive report in recent years, also found that income inequality in the UK had reached the highest since just after the Second World War. The report – *An Anatomy of Inequality in the UK* – establishes that 'who you are affect[s] the resources and opportunities available to you'. It links earnings, incomes and wealth with a range of social characteristics such as gender, ethnicity and age.

**Key findings of the Hills Report are:**

- Household wealth of the top 10% of the population, excluding bankers and chief executives, is 100 times higher than that of the poorest 10%.
- If bankers and chief executives are included, the top 1% then possess wealth of £2.6 million or more each on average.
- Wealth levels affect life expectancy.
- People's origins affect their occupational and economic destinations.
- Social class affects a child's readiness to go to school and a lower-social class background can 'drag them back' throughout their schooling and beyond.
- Economic advantages and disadvantages are reproduced and reinforced from one generation to the next.

## Housing

Data published by the ONS (2010) show that patterns of home ownership are linked to social class; for example, 92% of social class 1 either owned homes outright or with a mortgage, compared to 14% of the long-term unemployed and those who had never worked in social class 8.

Research by Le Grand (1998) and more recently organizations such as the Joseph Rowntree Foundation (www.jfr.org.uk) and the Child Poverty Action Group (www.cpag.org.uk) has highlighted the effects of poor housing on people's life chances. Damp, overcrowded and inadequately heated accommodation leads to inequalities such as physical and mental health problems, **educational underachievement**, reduced life expectancy and **social exclusion** (for example, children being unable to invite friends to their house).

**Essential notes**

Income is the amount an individual earns or receives in benefits. Wealth is income plus everything else deemed to be of value that a person owns.

## Social class and inequality: education and health

### Education

Working-class children do less well than their middle-class peers at every stage of education and the gap in achievement levels is increasing.

Archer et al. found that many working-class children do not aspire to go to university. Although the pupils in her study did not use Bourdieu's concepts of **social capital** and **cultural capital**, their views reflected them.

### Key study

Archer et al. carried out research in six London schools using mixed methods: structured and unstructured interviews, discussion groups and photographic diaries. They found that working-class pupils were able to overcome the sense of worthlessness they might have felt by adopting the style of the street. The style of the urban working-class youth was more important to them than university which, they said, was not what people like them aspired to.

The researchers needed to develop a **rapport** with the pupils in order to gain their trust and obtain valid in-depth data. Using unstructured methods of data collection helped this relationship as well as allowing the data to be cross-checked, increasing its validity.

Social inequalities linked to education include:

- the percentage of 16 year olds gaining 5 A*–Cs at GCSE is much higher for those from social class 1 compared to 6, 7 and 8
- approximately 7% of children go to private schools, 45% of whom go to Oxbridge
- children from classes 6, 7 and 8 are more likely to leave school at 16 than their counterparts in classes 1, 2 and 3
- Furlong and Cartmel (2005) found that working-class pupils who go to university tend to go to the 'new' ones and when they graduate tend to do less well in the labour market
- Feinstein (2003) argues that by the age of three children from working-class backgrounds are behind their middle-class peers by 22 to 42 months. In 2010 the Sutton Trust found the gap had narrowed slightly, from 11 to 16 months' difference between children from the poorest 20% of households and those from the middle 20% to richest 20%
- the number of books a child had in their home was more important in terms of the years a child remained in education than whether their parents had been to university. As few as 20 could have a negative impact whilst around 500 could lengthen a child's education by up to three years
- Hirsch (2006) argues that many working-class homes are unable to provide the same level of support as middle-class homes with regard to formal learning, even though they are loving and caring. It is the lack of **material resources** that disadvantages these children.

## Health

Health is also related to class inequalities.

- In 1980 the Black Report concluded there was a strong correlation between health and class.
- Reports by Whitehead (1992) and Acheson (1998) identified a similar link.
- The most recent government review of evidence of health inequality, the Wanless Report (2002), also found a clear link.
- Bottero (2005) argues that the link between health and class is self-evident given that rates of morbidity and mortality are not randomly distributed across the UK but are higher for the working class. This includes cancer, infections, coronary heart disease, strokes and accidents.
- The relationship between income inequality and poor health, including shorter life expectancy, is also noted by Wilkinson and Pickett (2009). Life expectancy is 78 for men in middle-class areas and 76 for men in poor areas. The gap for women is three years (National Audit Office 2010). Infant mortality is 50% worse in the north (Leeds) compared to the south (Dorset).
- Large-scale research on civil servants (Marmot, 1991, 2004) found people near the bottom of the hierarchy had the worst self-reported ill health, suffered greater stress and had higher levels of high blood pressure and depression than those at the top. Marmot found what he called a 'health gradient'; the lower down the hierarchy a person is, the worse their health.

## Evaluation

- Shaw (1999) agrees that material factors such as poor working conditions, an inadequate diet and bad living conditions are a major cause of ill health and those in social classes 6, 7 and 8 accumulate a range of these disadvantages over their lifetime. However, she argues ethnicity and gender are also factors causing ill health.
- Jackson and Wistow (2009) point out that although ethnicity, age, gender and housing are important determinants of health inequalities, it is class which is one of the major causes of the differential in health outcomes.

**Examiners' notes**

Remember to use examples from areas you studied at AS such as families and households, as well as from education or health, to illustrate social class inequality. Consider, for example, the differences between middle-class dual career families and working-class families, where the combined income of the working-class family is likely to be much lower than that of the middle class family, even if all the adults in a household work.

**Essential notes**

**Discrimination** is the unfavourable treatment of an individual or social group compared to other individuals or social groups.

**Essential notes**

There are several pieces of legislation you should be aware of:

- The 1970 Equal Pay Act enacted in 1975
- 1982/1985: two laws which strengthened the Equal Pay Act
- 1975 Sex Discrimination Act
- 2006 Equality Act, enforceable from 2010.

**Examiners' notes**

Use appropriate sociological terminology. **Sex** is a biological construct, gender is socially constructed. Sociologists usually use gender. Gender refers to men and women and therefore answers to exam questions which refer to gender must consider men and women.

**Essential notes**

The 'leaky pipeline' refers to the gradual loss of women in higher levels of an occupational area, and the '**concrete ceiling**' to the experiences of black and Asian women who are not told about the opportunities they might aspire to, and therefore cannot see through a 'glass ceiling'.

# Gender and inequality

Legislation over the last 40 years has failed to eradicate gender inequalities and discrimination in society. Gender inequalities can be found in areas of society such as the labour market, education, health and families and households. The extent to which women and men from different ethnic groups and social classes experience inequalities varies and it is not possible to make generalizations.

## Employment

- Women form 45% of the workforce but 40% of them work part-time, compared to only 11% of men.
- The rate of unemployment for women is rising faster than for men and reached one million in 2010.
- Single parents are more likely to be unemployed than married mothers.
- Women have, until recently, been the main carers of children, and with the ageing population many women in their 50s undertake 'dual caring', of both the elderly and children. However, men are now doing almost as much (Carers UK 2007).

## Horizontal segregation

This is the extent to which men and women are employed in different occupational groups.

- There are approximately 77 occupational groups and women are disproportionately clustered in the '5 cs' cleaning, caring, cashiering, catering and clerical (Women and Work Commission 2006).
- These five areas have significant numbers of low-paid, low-status jobs, many of which are part-time.

## Vertical segregation

This is the extent to which men and women are at different levels in occupations or in the labour market generally.

- There are large numbers of women in nursing and primary education, but only a relatively small percentage have the higher-status or better-paid jobs such as senior nurses or head teachers.
- In 2009 women constituted 12% of the directors of the top 100 FTSE companies (Cranfield School of Management). This rose to 13.6% in 2010. In an attempt to break the glass ceiling, which for some women is more of a 'concrete' ceiling, the directors of leading companies have set up the 30% group (2010).
- Women experience the '**leaky pipeline**' in some areas of employment, particularly those in science and technology where there are a lot of high-status, well-paid jobs.

## Gender pay gap

- The average pay gap between men and women is 16.4%.
- This can affect pensions and lead to the feminization of poverty amongst the elderly.

- The gender pay gap is lowest for people under 30; for those in their 40s it is on average five times greater (Equality and Human Rights Commission, 2010). In education the gap is 12.9% whilst in banking and finance it is 37.8%, reflecting the higher status of that sector.
- For disabled men the pay gap between them and other male workers is 11%; for women it is 22%.

## Education

- Girls of all ethnic backgrounds do better than boys.
- Girls from Chinese and Indian backgrounds do better than any other social group.
- Subject choices are gendered; for example, physics is male-dominated.
- The number of boys excluded, especially black boys, is four times that of girls.
- Girls are more likely to self-exclude by truanting (Osler and Vincent, 2003).
- Archer (2003) found that some Asian boys are becoming as disruptive as other boys, in her study *Race, Masculinity and Schooling*.

### Key study

Using qualitative methods of data collection, Francis (2000) studied 14–16 year olds in three schools. She found that schools were male-orientated and boys tended to dominate the classroom, often with noisy and disruptive behaviour. Boys also dominated the playground by occupying space. She found that some teachers treated boys and girls differently and in some cases disciplined the boys more harshly. The disruptive behaviour of girls was much quieter and therefore less noticeable. Francis found that girls received less attention from teachers than boys, partly as a result of the different behaviours. Consequently they were disadvantaged by not being pushed to their full potential.

**Source**: Francis, B. (2000) *Boys, Girls and Achievement: Addressing the Classroom Issues.*

Jackson (2006) found there had been a shift in girls' behaviour; some were adopting **laddish** behaviours traditionally associated with boys, becoming **ladettes**.

## Health

- Women have longer life expectancy than men, 82 years compared to 78, but the gap is closing (Department of Health, 2010).
- Women experience greater morbidity, including more stress-related illnesses.
- Women use health services more but that is inflated by pregnancy, care of children and their longevity.
- Men are more likely to be alcoholics and drug users.
- Young males engage in risky behaviour (**edgework**) increasing the risk of accidents or death (Lyng, 1990), but girls now join the boys in weekend binge drinking and violence (Winlow, 2007).

### Essential notes

**Mortality** statistics refer to death rates, **morbidity** statistics to illness.

### Essential notes

Researchers at the University of Leeds have predicted that figures for minority ethnic groups will rise after data from the 2011 census is analysed, with some groups such as the Irish growing fairly slowly whilst 'other whites' (people from the EU, US and Australasia) will be growing the fastest.

### Examiners' notes

The use of the term '**race**' is problematic and therefore most sociologists use ethnicity. When collecting data the government also uses ethnicity.

### Examiners' notes

There are as many differences in terms of power and status between ethnic groups as there are similarities; sweeping generalizations about all minority ethnic groups should be avoided.

**Source**: Bhopal, K. (1999) *South Asian Women Homeworkers in East London* in Gregory et al. *Women, Work and Inequality* (Macmillan, 1999)

### Essential notes

The term **ethnic penalty** describes the disadvantages minority ethnic groups face in the labour market compared with whites of the same age and with similar cultural and social capital (Yi Cheung, 2006).

## Ethnicity and inequality

### Ethnicity

**Ethnicity** refers to a person's cultural background including their values, traditions, customs, and language. The UK minority ethnic population makes up 7.9% of the total (census, 2001).

Minority ethnic groups often experience discrimination in areas such as education, employment, housing and health.

### Employment

- Chinese and Indian men earn more than any other ethnic group and are more likely to enter the professions. Bangladeshi men and women are the lowest paid (Hills Report, 2010).
- The unemployment rate of black graduates is 24%, worse than any other group of graduates.
- Hills et al. (2005) found there was a high level of unemployment amongst Pakistani and Bangladeshi men.
- Yi Cheung (2006) points out that the proportion of young people entering the labour market from minority ethnic groups is much higher than for the white population because of the younger age profile. However, she argues they can experience the '**ethnic penalty**'.
- Women workers from Pakistani and Bangladeshi backgrounds are sometimes limited by **cultural constraints** (Bhopal, 1999).

Bhopal's study in East London found evidence of the relationship between ethnicity, class and gender in the employment situation of South Asian homeworkers.

### Key study

Bhopal studied South Asian homeworkers in East London. She used qualitative methods of data collection, interviewing women in their own homes to find out why they had become homeworkers, how they felt about the conditions under which they worked and the choices they had. She defined homeworkers as people working from home on low pay, with few if any rights. She found that all the women had arranged marriages, and they worked at home because either their husbands preferred it or they wanted to look after their children while they worked. Their wages were extremely low, but despite that, some of the women said being a homeworker gave them "... the best of both worlds ... we are working and we are looking after our family" (Meena). On the other hand, some felt isolated and lonely and had become depressed. They also suffered from other health problems such as backache.

### Education

Education is seen as a means for social mobility, but that has not been the experience of all minority ethnic groups.

- Pakistani and black students do least well in the education system.
- Black students are more likely to be excluded or labelled as troublesome and loud.

However:

- students from most minority ethnic groups remain in education longer than their white peers
- minority ethnic students are entering higher education at a higher rate than their white peers, although they tend to go to the 'new' universities.
- those from poor backgrounds, measured by entitlement to free school meals, do better than their white peers.

## Health

Members of minority ethnic groups die of the same range of diseases as those from the majority ethnic group. There are some variations, although Nettleton (1995) argues that these must be viewed with some caution, especially when class is taken into account. Field and Blakemore (2003) agree but argue that there are some clear patterns of health and illness which are different from the majority white population.

- The risk of poor health and higher mortality is greater in most minority ethnic communites than in the white majority, with the exception of Indian and African-Asian communities. Both have better health than that of the white majority.
- Most minority ethnic groups suffer less lung cancer and breast cancer than the white majority and are less subject to illnesses connected to the respiratory system.
- Africans and African-Caribbeans have an increased incidence of high blood pressure and strokes.
- Indians, Pakistanis and Bangladeshis are more likely to have diabetes, TB and liver cancer.
- Pakistanis and Bangladeshis are more likely to suffer from coronary heart disease.
- African-Caribbeans are more likely to be compulsorily sectioned under the Mental Health Act.
- African-Caribbean and Pakistani babies are twice as likely to die in the first year of life as Bangladeshi and white babies (EHRC 2010).
- People from the Indian sub-continent tend to consume less alcohol and have lower rates of smoking.
- Men and women from the Pakistani and Bangladeshi communities as well as African-Caribbean women are more likely to report bad health than any other group.

## Housing

- Many minority ethnic groups, who are also working class, suffer the same poor housing deprivations as the white working class (damp and overcrowded) and 40% of minority ethnic groups are in non-decent housing compared to 32% of the white majority (English House Condition Survey 2001).
- Pakistanis and Bangladeshis are more likely to live in deprived inner-city areas in poor housing than any other group (Pilkington, 2005).

**Examiners' notes**

When making the link between ethnicity and inequalities remember to point out how, as in Bhopal's study, it intersects with gender and class.

## Essential notes

Differences can be found across societies; for example, children in the UK are not permitted to work full-time until they are 16 but worldwide there are 1.5 million children between 5 and 14 working full-time.

## Essential notes

There are some similarities in the ways in which the young and elderly are treated and some of these lead to stereotypes:

- vulnerable and in need of care and protection
- low status
- having less power than other population groups.

## Essential notes

The **feminization of the elderly** is partly a result of women's longer life expectancy and partly the loss of numbers of men who would by now be in this age-group but died in the Second World War.

## Essential notes

Life expectancy refers to how long someone born in a particular year can expect to live.

## Essential notes

Pensionable age in the UK is rising to 66+. From 2011 an employer cannot force an employee to retire. Some professionals such as judges and GPs can already choose when to retire.

# Age and inequality

The meanings attached to stages of a person's life-course vary; what it means to be young, middle-aged or elderly is **socially constructed**.

## Demography

The population of the UK is approximately 62 million, almost 20% of whom are under 16, while just over 20% are 60 plus. The birth rate has started to rise, but the over-85s are the fastest growing age-group. The percentage of women in this group is higher than men.

## The elderly

The United Nations defines elderly as 60 plus.

Milne and Harding (1990) studied the lifestyles of over 1 000 people and found two elderly worlds, the 'young elderly' and 'older elderly'. As people live longer, their expectations of when to retire and perceptions of themselves as 'elderly' change. Age tends to exacerbate existing inequalities of gender, class and ethnicity, and retirement can bring loss of status and power. The elderly non-productive are increasing, although many are taking on childcare roles, enabling their children to be productive.

### Economic factors

**Fuel poverty** affects over 1.7 million pensioners (Age Concern 2010) and the Child Poverty Action Group (CPAG, 2009) estimate that over two million are below the poverty line.

Giddens (2006) argues that 18% of pensioners live in poverty compared to 7% of the working population.

The costs of health care increase with age and Greengross (2004) argues that the elderly are penalized in relation to travel insurance and loans.

**Material deprivation** is worse for older women than men and they are likely to have smaller pensions than men, while some minority ethnic groups, particularly Pakistanis and Bangladeshis, may not have an occupational pension (Ginn, 2001).

Those who bought property in their 20s are often 'equity rich but income poor' (Davidson, 2006). They own a house but much of their income is spent on mortgage repayments.

### Health and care

Many elderly people experience life-limiting illnesses such as arthritis. The increase in the numbers of the elderly has increased health care costs and led to a view of the elderly as a burden. Greengross notes there is some evidence of institutional ageism in the NHS. Geriatrics is viewed as a low-status specialism.

The elderly who need care are often reliant on younger women. The EHRC found that the ageing population is creating a new kind of 'chronic disadvantage' as many middle-aged couples struggle to care for elderly relatives as well as children (2010).

Arber et al. (2006) found that older men on their own often delay going to the doctor. Older divorced and never-married men are more likely to indulge in a poor diet and smoke.

## Employment

Some of the inequalities faced by the elderly are a result of **age discrimination**. One in five workers experience discrimination, and 38% of them said that ageism was the reason (MORI 2002). However, some companies, such as B&Q, have a positive commitment to the employment of older or retired people.

## Young people

During the last 50 years legislation has sought to control children's lives and protect them. Gittins (1998) describes this as **age patriarchy**.

## Economic factors

There are 2.8 million children living in poverty in the UK (CPAG 2009). Many young people who are working are paid the minimum wage. Young people leaving university have large student loans and graduate employment is low.

## Education

There are barriers to continuing education. For example, Midgely and Bradshaw (2006) found that access to post-16 education and training differs in rural and urban areas.

Increased student fees may deter some young people from going to university, while graduate unemployment rose from 7.9% in 2009 to 8.9% in 2010.

### Key study

Using focus groups and interviews Midgely and Bradshaw studied the barriers and opportunities available to 16–19 year olds in rural areas as they left full-time education. They found that the options were limited as 'specialized diplomas' and other training courses were not available, and job opportunities were scarce in the rural areas. The young people could not afford to move to cities where there were courses and jobs. Midgely and Bradshaw argue that these young people would end up as NEETS.

## Social exclusion

In areas of high unemployment young people may be excluded from mainstream society (McDonald and Marsh, 2005), while the increase in NEETS has the same effect.

## Health

Children from low income families are more likely to die at birth or go on the child protection register (Howard, 2001), and are 2.5 times more likely to suffer from chronic illness (Millennium Cohort Study, 2008).

There has been an increase in certain diseases in young people; for example, chlamydia rates have doubled from 1999 to 2008 (NHS, 2009).

### Essential notes

Ageism is the unfair treatment of a person or group compared to another because of age.

### Essential notes

Age patriarchy is control of children by adults, a reinforcing of the inequalities between adults and children.

**Source:** Midgely, J. and Bradshaw, R. *'Should I Stay or Should I Go?' Rural Youth Transitions* (IPPR and CRC, 2006)

### Essential notes

NEETS are young people not in employment, education or training.

### Examiners' notes

Make sure you revise your AS notes for examples on age inequalities in all areas, including those on youth and youth subcultures.

## Functionalist explanations of inequality

Functionalists argue that inequalities have a purpose: they are functional for society. Functionalism is a **structural theory** based on the notion that society is based on **shared values**. This **consensus** means that society will be in a state of equilibrium and there is harmony, as a result of which there will be **social solidarity**. Inequalities, functionalists argue, exist in all societies and are inevitable and necessary.

### Durkheim and inequality

Functionalism has its roots in the work of 19th-century sociologists, in particular Durkheim.

Durkheim argued that:

- Industrialized societies are complex.
- Society needs specialists to undertake the various jobs and roles required to make it run smoothly.
- This harmony could be achieved by a division of labour whereby people have different jobs.
- Some of the jobs would have a higher status than others and greater rewards and power.
- People would accept this as long as they could see that the system was fair.
- Conflict might occur but it could be controlled by socialization.
- Socialization was the process whereby shared values could be passed from one generation to the next. At the time Durkheim was writing he argued that education, the family and religion were three of the important agents of socialization.
- Disharmony might arise when people felt the system was not fair, for example, when large bonuses are paid to bankers during a recession.

### Parsons and inequality

Parsons was a leading structural functionalist writing in the 20th century who developed Durkheim's ideas. He said that:

- In industrialized societies stratification, and therefore inequality, exists on the basis of which roles are agreed to be the most important, and therefore the most functional for society.
- The agreement occurs because people are socialized into the shared norms and values of society, initially by the family, and subsequently by education and other agents of socialization.
- The value consensus that results is what holds society together and it gives it social order. Sharing a common identity gives people a sense of purpose and a commitment to the maintenance of society.
- These values also give people common goals such as to work hard.
- People have a number of roles, an example being the expressive roles that women are most naturally suited for and the instrumental roles of men. These roles are ascribed rather than achieved.

## Examiners' notes

It is important to understand the theoretical debates between, for example, the consensus view as expressed by functionalists, and the conflict view of the Marxists, and the macro/structural view of functionalists and Marxists as opposed to the micro view of social action theorists such as the Weberians.

## Essential notes

Durkheim used the concept of a collective conscience, which, he said, was the common beliefs and values of a society.

## Essential notes

Social stratification is the way in which societies are layered, with some groups being ranked above or below others. These groups will usually share interests and have common lifestyles based on their cultural, social and economic capital. Functionalist sociologists tend to refer to stratification rather than class.

## Davis and Moore and inequality

Two other functionalists, Davis and Moore, have built on the ideas of Parsons and Durkheim.

- They argue that society needs the most talented people to perform the most skilled jobs and therefore has to pay them accordingly and give them high status.
- There is a meritocracy and the most able will, through the examination system, be allocated to the most important jobs. Their class position will reflect this role allocation.
- There is an expectation that the most talented will be prepared to make sacrifices early on in order to be educated and trained, and for this they will be rewarded later.
- The examination system will 'sift and sort' people into appropriate jobs. This means the system is legitimated.
- The stratification that results will ensure those at the top work to maintain their position and those lower down try to better themselves.

## Evaluation of functionalist explanations of inequality

- People do not all start from the same point, therefore a true meritocracy is not possible.
- Society is not harmonious. There is evidence of conflict between social groups in the form of strikes as well as disaffection amongst, for example, young people who cannot get work.
- Differences between men and women are socially constructed.
- There is not a consensus with regard to which are the most important jobs; for example, bankers are paid very well but most people would probably argue nurses are more important to society.
- Some groups start with more power and status and are therefore able to ensure they and their children get access to the education that will mean they then get the higher status jobs.
- **Life chances** are affected by status and wealth and the poor have less access to opportunities to gain status and wealth.
- Tumin argued that going to university is not really a sacrifice, although many people in the UK would probably argue it will be as fees go up.
- Merton argues some aspects of society are dysfunctional.
- The work of the functionalists is not supported by empirical evidence, particularly with regard to the idea that there is a value consensus.

### Essential notes

Davis and Moore called this sifting and sorting 'role allocation'.

### Examiners' notes

The New Right, who emerged in the 1990s around the politics of Thatcher and Reagan, agree with some of the functionalist ideas about society. They argue that there is a meritocracy, but that some people are not motivated to work hard and do their best and as a consequence may end up in low-status jobs or as part of the underclass.

### Essential notes

Basic needs are food, shelter and water. Marx said that the economic arrangements people make to meet these needs is the mode of production which, in the UK, is capitalism. Understanding how a society organizes itself to meet their basic needs is the key to understanding the structure of the society.

### Examiners' notes

Marx identified a range of other classes, including students, academics, the petit-bourgeoisie and the lumpenproletariat. It is important to avoid suggesting there were two classes: there were two main classes.

### Essential notes

The ruling class are the dominant group who are essentially the same as the bourgeoisie. They have the ability to control politics as a result of their ownership of the means of production.

### Essential notes

**Alienation** is another Marxist concept. It means the way in which workers experience their work as separate from them, not something they feel satisfies their inherent creativity. The product of their labour belongs to someone else.

## Marxist explanations of inequality

Marxism is based on the writings of the 19th-century philosopher and social economist Karl Marx. He argued that economic forces shape society and 'the history of all hitherto existing society is the history of class struggles'. (Communist Manifesto, 1848)

This is a macro theory which, like functionalism, is concerned with the structure of society. Marxism explains inequalities in societies such as Britain by examining the ways in which the **bourgeoisie** exploit and oppress the working class or **proletariat**. Inequalities are a result of the economic arrangements people make to meet their basic needs.

- A few wealthy and powerful people, the bourgeoisie, own the means of production and the rest just own their labour power. This creates a major division in society between the bourgeoisie and the proletariat and is a potential source of class conflict.
- The means of production are land, raw materials, factories and machines.
- The bourgeoisie exploit and oppress the proletariat.
- They exploit them by keeping wages as low as possible.
- The proletariat are much larger in number than the bourgeoisie, but because they own nothing but their labour power they are mostly dependent on the bourgeoisie.
- The proletariat have little or no power, whereas the bourgeoisie have the power to exploit and oppress the workers they employ in order to obtain surplus value or profit.
- Order and stability exist in society because the ruling class exercise power over all other groups. The elected government acts on behalf of the bourgeoisie; they implement laws to protect their property and determine working practices.
- **Capitalism** survives because the inherent inequalities are either not recognized or are accepted as just. People believe the system is fair.
- Marx argued if people did not recognize they were being exploited or thought it was just, it could be said they had a **false class consciousness**.
- One way in which the ruling class persuade people the inequalities are fair and just is via the various elements of the superstructure (the various agents of socialization such as the family and education).
- There are some who are aware of their exploitation; they have **class consciousness**, which means they know who the others are in their position and could act with them in opposition to the dominant group (for example, the miners in 1984).

### Bowles and Gintis

Many sociologiots have applied Marx's ideas for their analysis of different parts of society. Bowles and Gintis used Marxist ideas to explain how the education system reproduced the ideas of the ruling class and legitimated inequalities. They argue that:

- Students' experience of schooling is an **alienating** one.

- School specifically prepares students for their future as workers in a capitalist system.
- They argue that school does not prepare everyone in the same way; it prepares them according to their future position in society.
- They argue that schools are not meritocratic and that claiming they are is part of the ruling class **ideology** persuading people that inequalities are fair.

## Braverman

Braverman argued that inequalities in the workplace are exacerbated by certain factors.

- He argues that there has been **de-skilling** of white-collar jobs; they have become **proletarianized**. Technology has been one of the causes of this.
- He also argues that the same has happened to some professions. Teachers are an example. They are increasingly regulated and inspected. They are told what to teach and when.

De-skilling leads to a loss of bargaining power by the workers concerned and a consequent loss of earnings and conditions relative to others.

## Evaluation

- Marx argued that capitalism would eventually give way to socialism and then to communism, but it clearly has not and, despite various crises and recessions, it manages to survive.
- The New Right as well as functionalists argue that the bourgeoisie are not a united class.
- Postmodernists argue that class is dead and people make their own lifestyle choices now.
- Feminists argue that traditional Marxists ignore the gender inequalities women experience.
- The New Right argue that people make their own choices; they are not controlled by the ruling class.
- Not everyone has a false class consciousness; some understand only too well they are being exploited.
- Bowles and Gintis do not allow for exceptions; they take a very deterministic position.

**Examiners' notes**

It is important to use concepts such as:

- **proletarianization**, the process of a group becoming like the proletariat in terms of their social relationship with the bourgeoisie
- **de-skilling**, the loss of skills which then means employers have more power over the workforce

**Examiners' notes**

Ensure you draw on material from across the units you have studied and always evaluate one theory against others.

**Essential notes**

Neo-Marxists seek to explain the inequalities experienced by minority ethnic groups and women, who are largely overlooked by traditional Marxists.

**Examiners' notes**

The work of the neo-Marxists is particularly useful in explaining changing class and ethnic inequalities.

**Examiners' notes**

You could refer to this idea of Gramsci's in an essay on changing class structure.

**Essential notes**

**Ideology** is a set of 'false' beliefs which serve the interests of the ruling class and which justifies their dominance.

## Neo-Marxist explanations of inequality

Neo-Marxists have developed the ideas of Marx, taking account of changes and developments in the 20th century. They argue that the **infrastructure** (the economic base of society) and the social relations that arise from it are important in understanding inequalities, but so too is the role of ideas and culture.

Neo-Marxists have focused on a number of areas to explain inequalities including:

- the dominance of ruling-class ideas
- the relationship between the infrastructure and the superstructure
- the changing nature of the class structure
- the relationship between **cultural**, **social** and **economic capital**
- the role of the media.

### The dominance of ruling class ideas – hegemony

Gramsci (1971) stressed the role of ideas in enabling the ruling class to maintain its power and control. He argued that the ruling class spread their ideas through social institutions such as education, religion and the media.

- He used the concept of **hegemony** to describe the ideological control the dominant class have over the masses.
- He argued that the bourgeoisie control the working class by controlling ideas. The ideas of the ruling class have become the dominant ideas.
- Gramsci argued that the ruling class could not simply rely on the working class having a **false class consciousness**, since there was evidence to demonstrate many of them understood only too well the way in which they were being exploited and at times challenged it.
- Gramsci argued that there are divisions in classes and the state can exploit these divisions in order to maintain ruling class hegemony.
- Hegemony is a powerful way to control the working class; it persuades them that the **power** and rule of the bourgeoisie are legitimate.

### The relationship between the infrastructure and the superstructure

Neo-Marxists argue that the relationship between the economic base, or infrastructure, of a society and the superstructure is crucial in understanding the way in which the ruling class reproduce and legitimate class inequality.

- The infrastructure is the mode of production and social relations are inextricably linked to this.
- In a capitalist economy social relationships are articulated via money. The proletariat sell their labour power to the capitalists or bourgeoisie. In doing so they implicitly accept they will be exploited and oppressed.
- The superstructure reproduces the class inequalities located in the infrastructure and legitimates them by the transmission of the dominant **ideology**.

- Althusser (1970) argues the education system does this so successfully that the working classes accept the system is fair.
- Althusser argues that most ruling classes rely on the **ideological state apparatus** to persuade people that inequalities are fair, but the repressive state apparatus is always available if it proves necessary.

## The changing nature of the class structure

Wright (1978) argues that the growth of technology and of intermediate supervisors and managers has led to changes in the class structure.

- Control is now important as well as the relationship to the means of production. By control Wright meant control of labour, of investment and of the means of production.
- Some non-manual occupations are in a **contradictory class position**. They are between two classes, the one above having more control and the one below having less. Managers or those with substantial control are in a position to exploit others even though they themselves are exploited by the owners of the means of production.

## Cultural, social and economic capital

- Bourdieu argues that class inequalities are reproduced by the education system.
- The system values the **cultural capital** of the middle classes.
- They are able to impose their habitus on the education system; this then gives their children an advantage.
- Their academic success can then be translated into economic capital, for example, good jobs.
- The **cultural capital** they possess also allows them to introduce their children to the 'right' or influential people in the job market.

## The role of the media

The neo-Marxists of the Frankfurt school, including Marcuse, argue that the media diverts the attention of the working class from the inequalities they are experiencing and encourages them to consume and become involved in a celebrity culture. They also say that the media has an important role in controlling the working class, and persuades people to accept inequalities. Capitalism, they claim, has shifted the working class from a focus on economic inequality to consumerism.

In relation to the media, other neo-Marxists such as the Glasgow University Media Group argue that media professionals, editors and journalists reinforce the dominant ideology. These people come from the dominant white middle class and so for them it is the norm to select the news in the way they do, and it is not a conspiracy.

**Essential notes**

The repressive state apparatus is the forces of law and order and the armed forces.

**Essential notes**

**Cultural capital** is the experiences, language, values, skills, knowledge and lifestyles of the dominant group.

**Essential notes**

By habitus Bourdieu meant the ideas and cultural framework of a class. Children are socialized into the habitus of their class.

**Examiners' notes**

A useful evaluative point is that the arguments of the neo-Marxists and the neo-Weberians are to an extent similar.

## Essential notes

Weber was a social action theorist who wanted to understand the meanings people attach to their actions. He wanted to gain **verstehen**.

## Examiners' notes

Life chances are the opportunities a person has to have decent education, housing, health and employment. This is an important concept and can be used in other units such as education. Roker's study *Gaining the Edge* illustrates the opportunities middle-class girls whose parents sent them to private school had over grammar school girls from middle-class backgrounds. Their class was the same but, within the class, differences of income to afford fees gave the private school girls the edge.

## Essential notes

Weber identified four class groupings in capitalist societies:

1 the propertied upper class – the positively privileged
2 the propertyless white-collar workers
3 The petit bourgeoisie – the middle classes
4 The manual working class – the negatively privileged.

## Examiners' notes

Go back to your AS notes and remind yourself of the meaning of ascribed and achieved status.

## Weberian explanations of inequality

Weber was writing at the turn of the 19th century. He argued that stratification is not just based on the economic relationships people enter into, as Marx argued, but the standing or **status** a person has and the political influence or power a person might have as a result of membership of a political party or trade union. Class, status and party are all linked to power. However, he accepted that class is the most important determinant of the three in relation to the acquisition of life chances and inequality.

### Class

Weber and Weberians argue that class is concerned with the production of goods. It is concerned with the ownership or non-ownership of economic resources as well as occupational skills. A person's class is based on what they bring to the 'marketplace'. Those who own the most marketable resources, such as skills, education and income, will be able to acquire more income and access to life chances, giving them advantages in comparison to others. For example, parents with economic power can move house to live in the catchment area of a so-called 'good' school.

Homogeneous classes are not a given; rather, within a class there are several layers. Within a class there may be different levels of skills and power. A car mechanic is more skilled than a road sweeper. The former will probably earn more and have a higher status. However, if the skilled person was a car assembly line worker they may have more power than the mechanic in a small garage to join a union and improve their position.

People are in the same class if they have the opportunity to obtain the same advantages as others in that class. The opportunity might be through the job they have; for example, a barrister will have a similar opportunity to a hospital consultant and both will have greater opportunities than a manager in a factory. Within the class the social status of the barrister and consultant will be higher than that of the factory manager. People can move up and down social classes; they can be socially mobile. The middle classes are expanding and **polarization** between rich and poor has not happened.

### Status

Status is based on a person's social position, on their prestige or social standing. This is based on the perception of others and of what society generally deems to be of high standing. Some occupations have high status whilst others in the same class might have less status and more economic capital.

Status groups compete with one another and practise **social closure**. Crompton (1993) argues that the British ruling class do this. They work to preserve their market position and tend to socialize with those they consider to have the same status as themselves. Some status groups spend their money on lifestyles that reinforce their sense of belonging to a status group: on designer clothes, for example. Women and minority ethnic groups often have lower status than white males in the class they are located in.

## Party

Parties are groups or organizations such as political parties, trade unions or pressure groups where people come together to either compete for power or influence those with it. The more power a person has the more they are likely to have access to better life chances, but membership of a powerful organization does not necessarily confer the most power – wealthy bankers may still exercise power in opposition to government decisions on bonuses, for example.

## Evaluation

- Weberian explanations of inequality ignore the power of the bourgeoisie.
- Postmodernists dismiss Weberianism as another grand theory.
- Feminists argue that Weberianism still does not pay enough attention to women, although neo-Weberians Barron and Norris argue women are often located in the secondary labour market as a result of their relatively low status and lack of power.
- Difficulty of understanding boundary lines between classes.

## Some similarities and differences with Marxist analysis of class

- Weber agreed with Marx that ownership of the means of production is the most important factor in terms of economic rewards and life chances.
- Weber thought a class would be unlikely to become class conscious because of the many layers within it.
- Marxists argue status is much more aligned to class than Weber suggested.
- Weber argued the market value of the skills of those who are propertyless varies.
- The polarization of the propertied and propertyless is not happening.
- Political power is not only based on economic power. Inequality for Weber is based on the different life chances people have in the market place whereas for Marx it was about relations based on production.

### Essential notes

Rex and Tomlinson (1979) argued that there was a dual labour market and working-class members of minority ethnic groups were largely in the secondary labour market. This was partly to do with their ethnicity and the lower status that gave them, and partly their underrepresentation in trade unions and therefore lack of power. This leads, they say, to the development of a racialized **underclass**.

### Essential notes

Weber defined power as the ability of individuals or groups to persuade or make others do something even if they do not want to do it. A trade union might have the power to gain a wage rise even if the employer does not want to give it to them.

### Essential notes

When a class becomes class conscious it is prepared to act together to further the interests of the class.

### Essential notes

The NS-SEC occupational scale was designed by Goldthorpe and others and took account of status as well as occupation. (See page 7.)

## Postmodern explanations of inequality

Postmodernism emerged in the 1980s as a way of making sense of social and cultural changes taking place such as:

- globalization
- the shift from a manufacturing to a knowledge-based society
- technological changes.

Postmodernists argued that the world was becoming increasingly characterized by uncertainty and diversity which cannot be explained by the old grand narratives, that is, the traditional sociological theories.

The service sector is now bigger than the primary and secondary sectors. People do not see themselves in class terms; they construct their identities via the media and what they consume. For postmodernists the key to inequalities lies in the development of the post-industrial world and the fact that the production of knowledge has taken precedence over manufacturing.

### The importance of consumption rather than production

Waters (1997) argues that people are enticed by advertising to conspicuously consume and buy the image they want to portray. Baudrillard (1983) argues that as we consume more and more we are buying images. We move away from social relationships to relationships with what we consume. Consumerism is democratic; we can choose what we want. There is no single shared reality; inequality is about the different lifestyle choices people make and not their relationship to the old economic divisions of class.

Pakulski and Waters (1996) argue that class is dead; to be middle class in the 21st century might for some be the type of property they live in, for others the holidays they take, for still others, wearing designer clothes. People are no longer interested in the social and economic relationships of class. The elderly also make lifestyle choices about how they will consume the services on offer to them to satisfy their wants (Wilson, 1997).

### The ubiquity of the media

For postmodernists the media is central; it provides images that can be lived out. The media has led to a greater diversity by showing the range of what is available. People reflect what they see in the media in what they consume.

### Globalization

Bradley (1995) suggests that new identities are created by **globalization**; we are exposed to a range of identities and cultural groups. We can choose to be any one of them. She also argues people no longer see class as their main identity; it intersects with gender and ethnicity.

Hall (1996) argues that 'new ethnicities' being developed which are partly a result of globalization. A process of hybridization is taking place and is a force for social change. The norm for individuals is complex multiple identities which are constantly shifting and being contested.

### Essential notes

Postmodernists take the view that grand narratives, the overarching stories or 'metanarratives' as Lyotard (1984) called them, such as Marxism, functionalism and Weberianism, are no longer able to explain the social world. They argue there are a number of competing explanations for inequalities and no one explanation is more 'true' than another.

### Essential notes

Postmodern ideas also have implications for work. There is no longer a 'job for life'; for example, the closure of coal mines meant sons could no longer follow fathers down the pit and work there until they retired.

### Essential notes

Pakulski and Waters take an entirely theoretical approach and have little empirical evidence to support their arguments.

### Essential notes

Pilkington argues the three main features of modernity, the period before postmodernity, are the dominance of capitalism, the consolidation of the modern state and rationality.

## Changing identities

Inequalities are shaped by lifestyle choices and a 'pick and mix' culture in which people are constantly changing their identity. People are more concerned with personal identities than with the collective identities of class. These personal identities may be shaped by what they consume, by their gender, their ethnicity and their experience of living in multicultural societies. Inequality is a reflection of the decisions people make about their identities. Some identities have more status and prestige.

It is possible to have several different identities at the same time. Modood (2008) argues there is now a 'super-diversity' in the UK as a result of the range of ethnic groups that live in Britain.

Gilroy argues that one of the biggest barriers to change and ending inequalities based on ethnicity is racial solidarity; hybridization could overcome that barrier. Ethnicities are changing with the emergence of hybrid identities.

Featherstone and Hepworth (1999) argue that age is fragmented. There is no typical older person and Wilson argues to have an all-embracing 'big story' about the elderly as dependent is to fail to see the range of elderly people. Everingham (2003) argues that life courses do not follow a similar path as a result of individual choices people make; people have their own individual story.

## Evaluation

The following critical points have been made about postmodern explanations of inequality:

- Not all accounts of the world are equally valid; some are more valid than others.
- There are many people who live in the reality of poverty and cannot make lifestyle choices. Poverty is structural and constrains people with regard to the choices they can make.
- Postmodernism benefits the ruling class to retain inequality; thus, postmodernism is a view that suits them.
- Manufacturing is still important.
- It links to the work of some feminists who argue that some of the 'metanarratives' such as traditional Marxism have either ignored or trivialized gender inequalities.
- Traditional sources of identity such as class, gender and ethnicity are still important.
- It is not possible to change every aspect of one's identity; some, such as age, are ascribed.

### Examiners' notes

Choosing to have 'dreads' or be a 'goth' may give more or less status with peers or in the wider society. Try to give examples wherever possible.

### Essential notes

Gilroy argues it is important to note that minority ethnic groups have a range of experiences both compared to each other and within specific groups and should not be treated as an homogeneous group.

## Examiners' notes

Gender inequalities are experienced by men and women. Read questions carefully to check whether you are being asked about gender inequalities or inequalities specifically faced by women or men. In addition, questions will sometimes ask for sociological explanations and sometimes feminist explanations; again, read the question very carefully.

## Essential notes

Parsons argues that the family has two functions, socializing children and the stabilization of the adult personality. It is through the first of these that gendered roles are learnt.

## Essential notes

Hakim (2004) argues there have been improvements in opportunities for women. Her theory is described as 'preference theory'. Women can choose to have a career, look after children or a combination of the two. They can make a 'rational choice' and exercise a preference.

## Explanations of gender inequality

### Functionalism

Functionalists argue that gender roles in families are different, not unequal. The difference, Parsons argues, is that women are more suited to the 'expressive' role of caring and nurturing and men to the 'instrumental' role of the breadwinner.

Murdock supports this view, arguing that one of the four functions of the family is to educate children into the accepted norms and values of society, which includes their gender roles.

### Human capital theory

Some economists take a similar view, arguing that men have more human capital than women as far as work is concerned. They have a greater commitment to work, more experience and undertake more training. It is not surprising, therefore, that women will, on balance, be paid less and receive less training, and therefore have less chance of promotion.

### Marxism

Abbott and Wallace (2005) argue that Marx marginalized women in his analysis of capitalism.

Engels, Marx's colleague, argued:

- The role of the family is to maintain and reproduce the labour force in order to support capitalism.
- The nuclear family enables men to pass on their property. Men need to control women so they know who are their heirs.

### Dual labour market theory

The dual labour market theory has its roots in neo-Weberianism. Barron and Norris argue that:

- There are two labour markets: the primary one where jobs are secure, well paid and there are good working conditions; and the secondary labour market, characterized by lower paid jobs with less security, often part-time or temporary.
- Workers in the secondary labour market are easily replaced and employers can get away with paying them poor wages compared to those in the primary labour market.
- Women are more likely to be employed in the secondary labour market because employers think they are less interested in work than men.

The dual labour market theory has been criticized by Burchell and Rubery (1994), who argue that the division between primary and secondary labour markets is too simplistic. Their research revealed at least five divisions, and these were not all gendered.

### Liberal feminists

Liberal feminists want equal opportunities for men and women. They argue this can be done by legislation and by changing attitudes.

They argue that:

- Gender roles are socially constructed through the family, education and the media.

- **Socialization** or sex-role conditioning leads to gender inequalities. Women are socialized into passive or subordinate roles and men into dominant ones. Oakley argues that a process of **canalization** and **manipulation** socializes children into specific gender roles.
- Teachers and careers advisors perpetuate the view that women and girls will be good at certain subjects and occupations (Kelly (1987), Colley (1986) and Grafton (1987)).
- Girls are still steered towards or still choose gendered subjects.
- Oakley argues that the dominant patriarchal ideology means women are perceived as wives and mothers and therefore as secondary in the job market.

### Gender roles in the family

- There has been progress with regard to gender roles in the family; men are now doing more childcare and more domestic labour (Hauri and Hollingworth). Somerville (2000) argues that women are now better off; they can get divorced, have access to good jobs, obtain a good education and have control over their fertility.
- Things are changing, particularly for dual career, middle-class families.
- Wilkinson argues that there has been a 'genderquake' as the service sector has increased in size and women are being empowered.
- Lees and Sharpe both argue that women's position is changing. They have greater aspirations than they did in the 1970s.

### Key study

Based largely on a review of the work of other feminists, Somerville takes a liberal feminist stance and argues there is considerable evidence to show progress in the position of women. They have greater freedom to take on paid work even when married with young children. They have more choice about the type of relationship and living arrangements they enter into, and the rise in the number of work-rich families has led to more men taking on domestic responsibilities. She argues that there is still a culture of men working long hours and an expectation that women will take on a greater share of childcare and domestic labour, but if there were more family-friendly flexible paid employment opportunities, even greater equality could be achieved.

### Evaluation

Liberal feminism:

- does not take account of structural constraints women face in the workplace or of their class and ethnicity
- assumes socialization is a passive process and men and women accept what they are told
- is criticized by other feminists for working within the patriarchal system rather than challenging it
- tends to focus on the public sphere and ignore the private
- lacks a common theoretical basis – liberal feminists simply believe social change is possible.

### Essential notes

Patriarchy is male domination: a patriarchal society is one which is dominated by men in all areas.

### Examiners' notes

It is important to make links from one part of the unit to another and to other units – liberal feminism could be linked to the 'march of progress' theorists. (See page 34.)

### Examiners' notes

Do not confuse positive action with positive discrimination. Positive discrimination is illegal; positive action is concerned with ensuring everyone has the same opportunities to, for example, apply for jobs.

**Source**: Somerville, J (2000), *Feminism and the Family; Politics and Society in the UK and USA*, Macmillan

### Essential notes

Focusing on the public sphere means that liberal feminists have not addressed some of the family issues such as domestic violence, which affect women and, to a lesser extent, men. In addition, Marxist and radical feminists argue changes in the law are not enough. Patriarchy is still the dominant ideology.

☞ This topic continues on the next two pages

## Marxist feminism

Marxist feminists argue:

- Women's oppression is inextricably linked to capitalism.
- Women are exploited by capitalism at work and at home; at home they meet the needs of capitalism by reproducing the next generation of workers and looking after the current workforce.
- They absorb the frustration and anger of husbands who are themselves exploited at work (Ansley, 1972).
- Women are encouraged by the patriarchal ideology to believe the system is fair.
- Despite the advent of the '**new man**' and some shift in the amount of childcare and domestic labour men do, women still do the majority.
- At work they are low paid and form a part of the **reserve army of labour**; they are a cheap source of labour and can be brought in and out of the labour force as necessary. They are also more likely to be casual or part-time and non-unionized, which makes it easy to 'let them go' when a recession occurs.
- They tend to change jobs more frequently then men, as childcare demands.
- Sexism as well as racism keeps the working class divided.
- Doyal argues the NHS serves the needs of capitalism by ensuring a healthy workforce. She argues the health service is sexist and patriarchal.
- They argue 'power to the sisters must mean power to the class'; in other words, changes will only take place if men and women work together.

### Evaluation

- The reserve army of labour theory fails to explain the gendered nature of jobs.
- Radical feminists argue that Marxist feminists pay too little attention to **patriarchy**.
- Black feminists argue that Marxist feminists tend to ignore minority ethnic groups.

## Radical feminism

- Radical feminists argue that patriarchy is the oldest oppression; men exploit and oppress women.
- The family is the main source of this oppression and some argue that all-female households are the better option.
- Education contributes to patriarchal ideology by reflecting a masculine view of the world through the presentation of subjects and teacher behaviour towards girls and boys.
- They argue that male domination in society means women are oppressed and subjected to violence in the home and on the streets.
- Ehrenreich and English (1978) argue that medicine has historically controlled women.

### Evaluation

- Marxist feminists say it is not realistic for radical feminists to suggest not all women share the same or similar experiences; the labour market experiences of middle-class women and working-class women are very different.

## Essential notes

Kerr argued that women served three bosses: their boss at work, their husband in the home and their husband's boss.

## Essential notes

Women are cheap labour and, as Beechey and others have argued, are used as a reserve army of labour; occasionally in a recession they are used to replace more expensive male workers.

- Radical feminists ignore the extent to which progress or gender equality has been made.
- They are accused of ignoring the divisions between women in relation to class and ethnicity.

## Black feminism

- Much of the work of feminists in the late 20th century has ignored ethnicity.
- Some black feminists argue families provide support in a racist society. They argue that the relationship between black men and women is different from that between white men and women.
- Black women are marginalized, oppressed and experience racialization. Mirza's study on black girls found that they developed strategies for dealing with these disadvantages.

### Key study

Mirza (1992) combined a longitudinal survey approach with a school-based **ethnography** in her study of 62 young second-generation Caribbean working-class women, aged 15 to 19, and their white male and female peers. The study took place in two working-class schools in London and followed the girls as they moved from school into the workplace. As a group, the black females were the highest achieving group in the two schools; black males were the lowest achievers and the white males and females were in between.

Mirza found the black girls did not accept the negative, often racist, attitudes of teachers towards them and were very positive about their own cultural and racial identity. They challenged their teachers' low academic expectations of them but lacked power in the organization of the school hierarchy to be 'heard'. Mirza found that despite the unsatisfactory nature of the careers service and careers advice, the girls retained high aspirations in terms of the work they hoped to do after school. They were driven by what Mirza described as 'educational urgency', meaning they wanted to succeed against the odds.

**Source**: Mirza, H.S (1992) *Young, Female and Black*, Routledge

## Postmodern feminists (sometimes described as difference feminists)

- Take the view that there are a range of masculinities and femininities to 'pick' from.
- There is no one grand story to explain the oppression of women.
- There are differences between women which will affect the choices they make.

### Examiners' notes

Line these points with the more general ideas of postmodernism described on pages 26–27.

## Post-feminism

Post-feminists argue that gender inequalities have largely disappeared and there is no longer a need for feminism. Some post-feminists see feminism as a negative influence, encouraging women to be dissatisfied with their family life.

## Examiners' notes

When answering a question on ethnic inequalities try to avoid 'lumping' everyone together. The experiences of members of minority ethnic groups vary and so does the experience of men and women in the same group.

## Essential notes

This was known as the immigrant-host model. Some aspect of this model is embedded in the Britishness test that those applying for citizenship must now take.

## Examiners' notes

Ensure you draw essays to a conclusion, especially when you have been asked to evaluate theories or explanations. There are similarities between the ideas of the Weberians and the neo-Marxists and you should draw these out in a question on ethnic inequalities.

## Essential notes

**Racism** takes a variety of forms from bullying to name calling and more violent attacks on individuals and groups. **Institutional racism** is the 'collective failure of an organization to provide an appropriate and professional service to people because of their colour, culture or ethnic origin'.

## Essential notes

Status inequality is the idea that people's position in society is more to do with

## Explanations of ethnic inequality

### Functionalist explanations

Functionalists argue that a stable society is based on shared norms and values, and when migrants come to a country they will eventually be assimilated and inequalities will lessen. Patterson (1965) espoused a similar view, adding that any racism from the dominant group was a result of 'ignorance and confusion; it was not deliberate and would eventually go'.

### Evaluation

- Solomos and Back (1994) argue **assimilation** does not lead to a decline in inequalities.
- Hall (1978) argued the immigrant-host model reinforced racism and inequalities because it defined minority ethnic groups as the problem and ignored structural inequalities.
- Functionalism fails to acknowledge that minority ethnic groups may wish to retain their own cultures and not be assimilated.

### Marxist explanations

Marxists argue that class is the most significant factor in explaining ethnic inequalities. Traditional Marxists (Westergaard and Resler, 1976) argue that the inequalities faced by members of minority ethnic groups are just the same as the inequalities suffered by the white working class. This is supported by Castles and Kosack (1973), who argue that racial prejudice enables the dominant class to 'divide' those who really have the same class interests.

### Evaluation

Solomos and Back (1994) argue traditional Marxism is inadequate in explaining contemporary issues of inequalities and power. There is no unified working class that opposes the capitalist class.

### Neo-Marxist explanations

Neo-Marxists argue that the traditional Marxist view is outdated, it is deterministic and does not take into account the racism experienced by minority ethnic groups.

Miles (1989) argues that the division between the ruling class and the working class is fundamental in a capitalist society, but racist ideology plays an important part in determining the position of minority ethnic groups within classes. He argues classes are racialized.

### Evaluation

Gilroy takes the view that 'race and class are separate but connected'. He argues inequalities are produced and then reproduced through, for example, the school system.

### Weberian/neo-Weberian explanations

Weberians argue that racial and ethnic inequalities are linked to economics but status and power are also important.

- Parkin (1979) argued class and status are equally important and the middle classes practise social closure to keep out people from minority ethnic backgrounds.

- Rex and Tomlinson argue there is a racialized underclass. They argue the marginalized position of many black and Asian people in the UK can be understood in terms of an underclass which occupies a disadvantaged position in areas such as employment, housing, education and power to make decisions.
- Barron and Norris argue there is a dual labour market: a primary sector with well-paid, secure jobs, and a secondary sector where jobs are less secure, often part-time, temporary and non-unionized. Minority ethnic groups are more likely to be in the secondary sector.

### Evaluation

- These views are similar to the neo-Marxist view in terms of **racialized class fractions**.
- New Right theorists such as Murray and Marsland argue many minority ethnic groups do not atttempt to engage with the labour market.
- The idea of a racialized underclass is not substantiated by evidence.

### Postmodernism

Postmodernists argue that we choose which aspects of each other's cultures we wish to have as part of our identity, and so inequalities between ethnic groups are complicated by hybridization.

Modood argues that what we now have is diversity and difference, and explanations for ethnic inequalities should focus on these and on identity. Given this development of hybrid cultures, Modood argues that it is difficult to analyse inequality by ethnic group; rather, it is easier to identify smaller groups to analyse.

### Evaluation

Marxists argue that postmodernists do not take account of the material deprivation that some minority ethnic groups experience, and that they focus more on culture and identity than inequalities.

their status than with their class. **Social closure** is a strategy used by one social group to exclude another, for example the use of the '**old-boy network**' in recruitment.

### Essential notes

This view of an **underclass** should not be confused with that of the New Right who take a 'blame the victim' approach to members of the underclass.

### Essential notes

Hybrid cultures/hybridization is the process whereby people from different ethnic backgrounds choose to take aspects of other people's cultures and hybrid cultures develop. Postmodernists use the concept of super-diversity to describe the cultural and ethnic diversity in the contemporary UK.

### Examiners' notes

Ensure you use appropriate terminology. Ethnicity is a complex issue and terminology is sometimes controversial. There are competing views as to the concepts that should be used. 'Minority ethnic groups' is currently used by a range of sociologists and government departments.

### Essential notes

The Equality Act 2010, which covers all forms of discrimination, came into force on October 1st 2010.

- - - - - - - - - - - - - - - - - - - - -

## Essential notes

The 'march of progress' theorists such as Ariès and Shorter argue that the position of children is a continually improving one; children are now protected against abuse, poverty and under-age work.

## Essential notes

There is no evidence that the elderly are as dependent as has been suggested, although some occupational pensions providers have announced they are struggling as the number of retired rises compared to those who are working and paying into the schemes.

## Essential notes

Phillipson (1982) argues that capitalism needs people to be 'useful' in terms of their labour power; it does not want people dependent on benefits.

## Essential notes

**Reserve army of labour** is a term used by Marxists to describe groups who can be easily moved in and out of the labour force as it suits the ruling class. These groups may include women, young people, older people and immigrants.

## Explanations of age inequality

### Functionalist explanations

- Parsons argued that social cohesion is based on age groups knowing their place and their roles.
- Children must be socialized into their adult roles. Eisenstadt agreed and argued that children have less status than adults. They must be taught skills and knowledge to enable them to perform their adult roles.
- The position of the elderly has improved with a statutory retirement age and a state pension, but they lose power and status as their children leave home and they retire.
- Older people need to 'disengage' from the workforce in order to make way for younger ones (Cumming and Henry, 1961). This ensures society is continually being 'refreshed'.

### Evaluation

- Age groups are not homogeneous. Young people do not always accept what they are taught; some rebel and join sub-cultures.
- Class affects the extent to which young and old are socially included in mainstream society.
- Hockey and James (1993) argue that functionalism is over-deterministic, emphasizing conformity and consensus; it fails to address inequalities which are a result of class, gender and ethnicity and seems to imply that the young rebel because society needs them to.
- 'Youth' and 'old age' are socially constructed and this serves to legitimate the separation of people by age and the resulting inequalities.
- Pensions create dependency and a fall in status.
- Hunt (2005) argues that the elderly do not automatically disengage; they may wish or need to continue working.

### Marxist explanations

- The inadequate state pension leads to some elderly people being dependent on benefits.
- Young people without skills and retired people form a **reserve army of labour**. Both groups have little power and it is easy to hire and fire them.
- The elderly tend to have less disposable income and are consequently of less interest to capitalism; they do not produce or consume.
- McDonald and Marsh (2005) found that young people in deprived areas lacked power and status.

### Evaluation

- Class divisions between youth subcultures are 'fleeting, fragmented and fluid'.
- The reserve army of labour theory does not explain age inequality. It can apply to social groups from any age.

- There is a growing number of elderly with disposable income who have 'consumer power'.

## Feminist explanations

- Oakley argues that inequalities experienced by children are inextricably linked to those of women and the patriarchal nature of society.
- Children are controlled by adults in relation to the age they can start work, their education, where they play and the use of their time. Some are controlled by abuse and neglect.
- Older women are materially deprived compared to men as a result of time out of employment and the gender pay gap (Gannon, 1999).

## Evaluation

- Wyness (2006) argues that children are controlled by both men and women.

The English Longitudinal Study of Ageing (ELSA) has identified age inequalities being experienced by the over 50s.

### Key study

The ELSA study (2008) found the poorest people had been affected most by price rises on food and fuel. They also found that working beyond the state pension age was linked to a higher level of education and good health. As far as the over 80s were concerned, women were more likely to have at least one physical limitation compared to men. The wealthier tended to consume more alcohol but ate a better diet and were less likely to be generally unwell.

**Source**: Institute of Fiscal Studies (2008), *The 2008 English Longitudinal Study of Ageing*

## Postmodern explanations

The social significance of age is changing. Age groups have become diverse and fragmented and boundaries are becoming blurred.

- Featherstone and Hepworth (1999) note there is a constant bombardment of messages from the media to try to 'stay young' and delay the ageing process. They call it the '**mask of ageing**'. On the other hand, children are being encouraged by the media to take on adult behaviours.
- The wealthier retired are described by Milne et al. (1999) as having '**grey power**', being conspicuous consumers.

## Evaluation

- Certain lifestyle choices, for example plastic surgery, may not be available to those with low incomes.
- Nayak (2003) argues that 'processes of class and racial disadvantage, and social and economic exclusion, impact heavily on youth leisure and culture'.
- Shildrick and McDonald (2010) argue that youth sub-cultures emerge as a response to material deprivation in areas such as Teesside.

## Essential notes

A QC is a barrister who has 'taken silk'. Until recently, QCs were selected by recommendation. Compared to an ordinary barrister, a QC can charge double for the cases they take on. QCs are usually educated at private school followed by Oxbridge. A well-known silk is Cherie Blair.

## Essential notes

Being accepted as upper class often requires 'breeding' and **cultural capital**, which, it is said, the 'nouveau riche' do not have.

**Source:** Lansley, S. *Rich Britain* Politico's Publishing Ltd

## Examiners' notes

**Elite self-recruitment** is the process whereby powerful jobs go to the children of the elite.

## The upper class

The upper class is the smallest social class. Its members are very wealthy and also often powerful. The upper class includes:

- The traditional aristocracy, the landed gentry and those with titles, including the royal family.
- The economic elite, many of whom appear on the *Sunday Times* Rich List. They are the people who have made their fortunes from industry, commerce and finance. Research by Adonis and Pollard argues that there is a '**super class**', by which they mean the **elite** of city financiers, QCs and company directors.
- Celebrities such as the Beckhams, Sir Paul McCartney and Simon Cowell.

### Questions with regard to the upper class

The points under each question list various arguments.

### Is the upper class in decline?

- Roberts argues that some of the traditional upper class have seen their wealth reduced as inheritance tax has risen.
- Scott (1997) argues that there is still an upper class and that they have better **life chances** than others and are generally advantaged. They own, Scott says, 'property for power', as opposed to 'property for use'. Most of the population have some of the latter, such as a house and car.
- Scott argues that a limited number of people sit on the boards of large companies – often more than one – and that this has led to the strengthening of the capitalist class.
- He argues that, in total, these successful directors and owners of large capital, together with those who have inherited wealth, comprise approximately 0.1% of the population.
- Lansley (2010) argues that despite a rise in the 'self-made super rich', for example, celebrities, tycoons and city dealmakers, birth is still the main determinant of the upper class. He argues that the upper class is not in decline.
- Adonis and Pollard (1998) argue that 'class divisions are intensifying'. This is based on their detailed evidence of inequalities, particularly in the education system and the employment that follows for those in the elite schools.

## Key study

Based on a wide range of secondary data, including official statistics, Lansley (2010) argues that there is a new super rich, comprised of bankers, tycoons and celebrities. However, despite the slight rise in the self-made super rich, birth still determines whether a person is regarded as being upper class or not.

### Is the upper class the ruling class?

- Scott argues that the upper class is also the ruling class, with 'political domination and power'.

- He argues that a 'power bloc' exists and from within that a 'power elite' emerge – people in powerful jobs such as cabinet ministers, senior civil servants and judges. They are in elite positions and act in a cohesive way, partly as a result of elite self-recruitment.
- They practise social closure by placing barriers in the way of those who attempt to be upwardly socially mobile and are a 'unified property class'.
- Rex (1974) argues that they are likely to have had similar school and university education and so are socialized into believing in the importance of acting together. Their common experiences legitimatize this common action.
- Westergaard and Resler (1975) take a Marxist position and argue that although the class system is complex, there is still evidence of a major division between capital and labour. This division is maintained by the ruling class, who act in the interests of capital.

**To what extent is the upper class influenced by the global economy?**
- Sklair (1995) argues there is a transnational capitalist class with increasing power. He cites a huge hamburger chain and a globally-known cola company as examples of the transnational companies these capitalists own and which give them global power. They make 'global' decisions and oppose tariff barriers.
- He argues that governments who try to make economic decisions without paying attention to these transnational capitalists may suffer from the withdrawal of their investments.

## Evaluation
- Saunders, a New Right theorist, argues that there is no ruling elite, but rather an 'influential economic elite'.
- He argues that old class divisions are much weaker, and though society needs inequalities, what has happened under capitalism is that wealth has spread to more people.

**Essential notes**

The educational background of the elites is inextricably linked to nepotism and the '**old-boy network**', and, increasingly, the 'old-girl network'.

**Essential notes**

Unlike the working class, it could be argued that the upper class have a clear **class consciousness**. They know how to act in the interests and maintenance of their class.

**Essential notes**

Sklair did not analyse the power of international banking, which, given the recent recession, could be argued to be somewhat of an omission.

## Essential notes

The reduction in manufacturing has occurred with the rise of cheap labour abroad and an increase in technology. Almost simultaneously, as the service sector has expanded, there has been a growth of routine white-collar work and an increase in professional and managerial jobs.

## Essential notes

Roberts (1977) argued that the middle class was becoming the middle classes as its range of jobs became more diverse and **fragmentation** occurred. Most sociologists refer to 'the middle classes', given the changes in the labour market and the diversity of employment that can be described as non-manual.

## Essential notes

The government's social mobility task force (2009) argued that the professions are becoming more, not less, socially exclusive.

**Source:** Devine, F (2004). *Class Practices: How Parents Help Their Children Get Good Jobs.* Cambridge UP

## Essential notes

In a life history interview the interviewer asks the interviewee about his or her life and relevant experiences. In Devine's case, she asked about education.

## The middle class

The shift from manufacturing to services has, over the last part of the 20th century and the start of the 21st century, led to growth in the middle classes. The middle class has historically been defined as those with non-manual jobs, which includes everyone from office workers to teachers. However, deciding who should be included and who should not is problematic and is known as the '**boundary problem**'.

### Who are the middle classes?

- Professionals, an educated skilled group of people with well-paid secure jobs, including doctors, lawyers and teachers.
- The self-employed, whom Marx referred to as the petit bourgeoisie.
- Managers, who have often risen through the ranks via promotion, and who do not always have professional qualifications.
- White-collar workers, including routine office workers.

### The professionals

The number of professionals has increased as the welfare state has grown and with it the need for a range of welfare professionals. Workers in many areas have sought professional status.

- Savage (1992) argues that professionals have **cultural** and **economic capital**, which enables them to ensure that their children go to good schools and get good jobs.
- Devine argues that middle-class parents pass on their values and cultural and social capital to their children in order to reproduce advantage.
- They can practise elite self-recruitment.
- Professional bodies such as the Law Society use examinations to socially exclude people.

### Key study

Devine carried out life history interviews in the UK and US with 86 parents of 116 children. She wanted to find out how middle-class parents 'mobilize their resources to help their children through the education system and into good jobs'. Devine found that the parents were using their economic and cultural capital to help their children to do well at school. She also found that their social relationships with others of the same class were extremely important, adding additional social pressures to achieve. These parents were keen for their children to socialize with other 'nice' children who wanted to succeed. Devine also found that the reproduction of advantage is not always easy when the economic and political climate is less favourable.

### Managers

This group is not as tightly knit as the professionals.

- Managers are likely to have less job security.
- They tend to be a less cohesive and more individualistic group than professionals.

- Most will have aspirations for their children, wanting them to have a university education.
- They tend to have economic rather than cultural capital, and can therefore buy some cultural capital for their children.
- Savage (1992) argues that many managers have been upwardly socially mobile.
- Some are extremely well paid, and part of the '**super class**' identified by Adonis and Pollard.

### The self-employed
- The self-employed are diverse – from plumbers and electricians to management consultants.
- The number of self-employed people has increased as technology has developed.

### White-collar workers
This group includes a range of people, from shop-workers and secretaries to call centre workers. Various studies argue that white-collar workers have routinized jobs, poor conditions and poor wages.

- Braverman, a Marxist, argues that some white-collar workers have become **proletarianized**, and that their work has become **de-skilled** and routinized.
- Westergaard and Resler, also Marxists, argue that in terms of conditions and wages, white-collar workers are more similar to the working class than to the middle class.
- Crompton and Jones (1984) are critical of many studies of white-collar workers for ignoring the position of women, arguing that 91% of their sample had no control over their work.
- Marshall (1997) studied men and women, and disputes Crompton's view that clerical work has been de-skilled.

### Evaluation
- The neo-Marxist, Wright, argues that capitalist societies are formed of two major classes, the bourgeoisie and the proletariat, and that while there are those in the middle in a **contradictory class position**, they are not a class as such, just groups of intermediary workers.
- Giddens argues that the middle class should include lower-level white-collar workers.
- Savage et al. (1992) argues that the middle class is fluid and that there are a number of divisions, based on property, organizational skills and cultural assets. This is more likely to lead to intra-class conflict than homogeneity.
- The number of new technology workers who have some autonomy over their work has grown.

**Essential notes**

Adonis and Pollard suggested that the super class could be seen as part of the upper-class propertied elite.

**Essential notes**

A rather dated, but worth noting, study by Lockwood (1958) said that clerical workers have not been proletarianized.

## The working class

Traditional Marxists argue that the working class is homogeneous, but evidence points to a division between the traditional working class and the new working class.

### The traditional working class

Many people argue that the traditional working class has declined in numbers with changes such as **post-Fordism**, new technology, **globalization** and the decline of manufacturing.

### Characteristics of the traditional working class

- close-knit communities
- 'jobs for life' such as coal mining and ship building
- traditional gendered roles (women do most of the domestic work)
- **hegemonic masculinity**
- sense of class, class consciousness and awareness of social inequities.

### Evaluation

- Lockwood (1966) found many of the characteristics mentioned, but his study is quite dated.
- Cannadine (2000) argues that this is rather a rosy picture of the traditional working class, who were not as united as the text implies. There were, for example, always those people who were prepared to break a strike.

### The new working class

Crewe (1983) and others such as Goldthorpe and Lockwood argue that the new working class tend to live in the south, work in newer manufacturing industries and are often not unionized.

### Characteristics of the new working class

- They tend to have instrumental attitudes to work, meaning they go to work for the money rather than for personal satisfaction. Westergaard argues that this demonstrates their sense of alienation and therefore their common experiences with the working class in general.
- They tend to focus on family rather than class, and do not have any substantial degree of class consciousness, as Savage and others found in their studies in Manchester and elsewhere.
- Fragmentation as a class with the advent of post-Fordism.
- The new working class are less likely to be in a union.
- They tend to have privatized family lifestyles, with families spending their leisure time together. They focus on family life rather than the community living, as found for example, in Bethnal Green in the south and older mining communities in the north.
- They tend to have greater affluence, meaning that they have the money to become home and car owners and go on holidays as a family.

## Essential notes

**Post-Fordism** is the replacement of mass production techniques such as assembly lines with changes in the organization of work, which require greater skill and flexibility from the workforce.

## Essential notes

Westergaard is a argues that class is still the over-riding division in society in relation to inequalities.

In addition, Roberts argues that, with the rise of new technologies, new jobs have emerged, but many people receive low pay and their work is routinized; people sit in front of computer screens day after day.

Two central concepts in understanding the structure of the working class, and in particular the new working class, are **embourgeoisement** and proletarianization.

The embourgoisement thesis is based on the work of Zweig (1961). Goldthorpe and Lockwood (1968) tested it on the affluent car workers of Luton. They found that, while the car workers had an affluent lifestyle, they had not become like the middle class; they retained a 'them' and 'us' attitude towards their employers. Later, Devine found evidence that the workers held traditional values and attitudes, although they were also consumer-conscious. There was a convergence between their lifestyles and those of the middle classes.

McDowell argues that young men entering the labour market find their masculinity compromised as most job vacancies are in the feminized service sector.

## Key study

McDowell studied young white working-class males with low educational achievements in Sheffield and Cambridge. Her aim was to investigate ways in which the debate about the so-called '**crisis of masculinity**' and the young men's views of their own masculinities affected their attitudes and aspirations as they moved into the labour market. She found they thought that the way to an 'acceptable and respected masculine identity' was through waged work. After two years, most continued to be employed in low wage, casual work with little chance of promotion.

**Source:** McDowell, L. *Redundant Masculinities: Employment Change and White Working Class Youth.* Blackwell

## Evaluation

- Marxists argue that there is still a unified working class.
- Braverman argues that de-skilling has led to the proletarianization of routine clerical workers, who are now part of the working class.
- Post-modernists argue that class is less important than consumption.
- Miles argues that ethnicity divides classes and that there are racialized class fractions.
- Savage (2001, 2005) found, though tentatively, that people did often align themselves with their class to give them some 'ordinariness' and 'normality'.
- Vincent et al. (2007) found that respondents in their study of working-class families and childcare in London wanted to be acknowledged as respectable working class rather than 'the roughs'.
- Roberts argues that, far from acquiring a class consciousness, the working class are becoming more disorganized.

### Essential notes

Atkinson (2009) interviewed working-class parents and found that they are likely to live near where they themselves grew up, work in manual jobs and send their children to local schools.

**Essential notes**

Marx used the term 'lumpenproletariat' to describe the group beneath the working class, who he said, were '... social scum, that passively rotting mass thrown off by the lowest layers of the old society.'

## The underclass

Various terms are used to describe social groups who have become separated from mainstream society: the poor, marginalized, socially excluded, the **lumpenproletariat** and the underclass.

The term 'underclass' is used by some sociologists to describe people who are 'structurally separate and culturally distinct from the regularly employed working class' (MacDonald, 1997).

The characteristics of the **underclass** are poverty, unemployment and marginalization.

Murray, a New Right thinker, described them as benefit dependents, scroungers, anti-social and 'dangerous'.

### Is there an underclass?

Giddens and Runciman argue that there is an underclass, which can be structurally identified. Murray also argues that there is a clear underclass.

However, Mann and Bagguley both argue that there is no identifiable stable group which could be called the underclass. There are too many people moving in and out of unemployment, not 'stable members of an underclass, but unstable members of the working class'.

Finally, there are those who argue that more research must be done before it can be said that there is definitely an underclass.

### The New Right and cultural underclass theory

Murray (1984) argues that an underclass has developed, with rising rates of illegitimacy, an increase in single parents, rising crime rates and young people who are not prepared to get a job.

Murray argues that young men from the underclass are 'essentially barbarians'. Young women are 'welfare-draining single mothers and young men are feckless and criminal.' He says that the criminal justice system is weak, the state is over-generous in the benefits it pays, young mothers have no need to be married because they receive good benefits, young men no longer have to commit themselves to employment as they have no family responsibilities, and traditional family values are being eroded.

Marsland supports Murray's view, arguing that people in the underclass are welfare dependants.

### Evaluation

- The New Right neglect social and economic factors that lead to poverty.
- Murray's evidence is based on a cursory visit to the north-east, not detailed research.

### Structural view

Those who take a structural view argue that inequalities have led to an underclass, rather than a lifestyle choice. They do not take a united view but all agree that the underclass exists for structural reasons of one type or another.

Giddens argues that those at the bottom form a distinctive class. He says they are disadvantaged compared to the working class in the labour market and have the worst jobs, if they get employment at all. He also says there is a dual labour market and workers in the secondary labour market have low paid jobs and poor security, and that women and people from minority ethnic groups are the most likely to be in the underclass.

However, Mann argues that there is no clear division between the primary and secondary labour market as Giddens suggests, and says Giddens' theory does not take into account gender and ethnicity. He argues that there is no underclass.

Although Westergaard (1992) once argued that the underclass were part of the working class, he now argues that changing economic circumstances have meant that there are people 'situated structurally below the traditional working class'.

Runciman (1990) argues that there is a seven-class system in the UK. He bases his model on the extent to which people have control, power and marketability. He argues that the bottom five per cent constitute an underclass. He also emphasizes people's roles and argues that those whose roles mean that they are unable to participate in the labour market and who rely on benefits are the underclass.

Craine carried out an extensive study on youth in Manchester and while they were clearly disaffected, disconnected and marginalized, he did not conclude that they were an underclass.

### Key study

Craine spent 10 years researching a group of 39 young unqualified school leavers in an inner-city area of Manchester. For five of those years he was a youth worker on the estate, giving him 'insider-status'. He used ethnographic methods: observation, interviews and some general 'hanging about'. Craine was specifically interested in youth transitions in relation to work and domestic and housing 'careers'. He found that the young people were moved from one training course to another and it was the uselessness of that, together with the lack of jobs, that meant some of them 'chose' alternative careers of single parenthood or crime, which were rooted in their material circumstances and resulting disaffection. It did not necessarily make them part of an identifiable underclass.

McDonald and Marsh (2005) also take the view that structural and **material deprivation** have resulted in groups of young people being marginalized and disconnected from mainstream society, which is not of their own choosing.

### Examiners' notes

This is another opportunity to demonstrate your skill at making links from one part of the unit to another. Barron and Norris argue that there is a dual labour market. (See page 28.) In addition, Rex and Tomlinson argue that there is a racialized underclass. (See page 33.)

### Essential notes

Runciman argues that a significant number of these people are women or from minority ethnic groups, although he says it is not their gender or ethnicity that means they are there, but their reliance on state benefits.

### Essential notes

Craine's work can be linked to marginalization and the way in which some social groups are marginalized in society, which does not necessarily mean they are part of an underclass.

**Source:** Craine, S (1997). *The 'Black Magic Roundabout': Cyclical transitions, social exclusion and alternative careers* in MacDonald, R (1997), *Youth, the 'Underclass' and Social Exclusion*. Routledge

### Examiners' notes

Make another connection here with the work of MacDonald and Marsh on Teesside. (See page 4.)

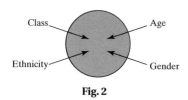

**Fig. 2**

## The relationship between class, gender, ethnicity and age

The relationship between class, gender, ethnicity and age is clearly linked to social difference as well as social inequalities. Two sociologists have contributed to the debate about this relationship:

- Devine (2005) argues that the intersection, or matrix, of class, gender and ethnicity is central to contemporary discussions of inequalities. However, she also says that it is problematic to assign people to fixed groups, since they belong to more than one group.
- Anthias (2004) argues that inequalities are not just about the separation of class, gender, ethnicity or age, but the ways in which these are interwoven.

### Evaluation

- Anthias argues '… it is not just that they intersect, but what is important, is how they intersect'.
- Bradley takes a postmodern view, preferring to use terms such as fragmentation and **hybridity** to try to reflect the flexible and dynamic social positions people occupy.
- Vincent et al. (2007), in their study on childcare in London, agree. They say, '… it is extremely hard to predict what areas of commonality and difference will exist between a white working-class, unemployed, young man in Rotherham, a white, middle-aged, skilled worker in Cheadle and a black, working-class mother with a clerical job in inner London'.

The point made by Vincent et al. highlights the complexities of the social characteristics of different people. Exploring the relationship between class, gender, ethnicity and age, without recognizing these complexities, is simplistic.

The relationship between class, gender, ethnicity and age occurs not just in terms of the social reality of the women, men and minority ethnic groups who are being studied, but also in relation to the researchers themselves, as shown by the following researchers:

- Gelsthorpe notes that the extent to which experience, age, sex and ethnicity can influence research is often ignored or underplayed. For example, during her study of male prisoners, she sometimes found that her gender was an issue.
- Phoenix, a black woman, carried out research on white women and found that the traditional power relationship in the interview was altered.
- Skeggs argues that class, gender, 'race', age and sexuality cannot be separated because people use those categories to help them organize their lives. Therefore, even if the researcher is from the same ethnic or gender background, class may affect his or her relationship with the person or people being researched.

We can use two studies to illustrate the relationship between class, gender, ethnicity and age.

1  During McRobbie's study of working-class girls, it was found that being female and having close female friends was most important to them. Class was less important.

## Key study

McRobbie found that being working-class meant little to the girls she studied. Being female was what was important to them. She studied 56 working-class girls aged 14 to 16. They had 'best friends' and this friendship was part of the **ideology of romance**. It involved being conscious of fashion and make-up and the idolization of male pop stars. McRobbie found that the girls faced a future of limited low-paid job opportunities and aspired to marry someone who was in a job that would enable them to make a life together. They were realistic about marriage but saw it as a way of gaining status in society.

2  Thiel, in his research of construction workers on a building site in London, found a 'highly masculine' dominant culture, which was also racialized.

## Key study

Thiel carried out an ethnographic study of workers on a London building site. He used **participant observation**, working as a labourer on the building site for a year. During the year, he observed the display of a number of aspects of working-class culture. For example, the workers enjoyed getting drunk and having a laugh, yet they distanced themselves from being identified as working class. Thiel found an 'ethnic hierarchy of labour', which meant that sub-contractors employed men from their own communities and only rarely hired outsiders. For example, the carpenters he observed had an Indian ethnic background and the labourers had an Irish background. Plasterers had a Seychellian ethnicity and managers were white British and lived in Kent.

He also found that the way the sub-contracting system of hiring builders worked meant that it was extremely difficult for migrant workers to get jobs on the site even though they were prepared to work harder for less money. When there was less work, migrant workers were always first to be laid off. These employment practices affected the employment opportunities and power of some minority ethnic groups in the labour market.

## Essential notes

A number of studies have shown that people tend to distance themselves from their class. For example, the young women Skeggs researched sought respectability, so they preferred not to be described as 'working-class'. To them, this would not be seen as being respectable.

**Source:** McRobbie, A (1977). *The Culture of Working Class Girls* in McRobbie (2000) *Feminism and Youth Culture*. Macmillan

## Examiners' notes

It is useful to keep your own list of studies in which the relationship between class, gender, ethnicity and age has been researched.

**Source:** Thiel, D (2007). 'Class in Construction: London building workers, dirty work and physical cultures' *British Journal of Sociology*

## Examiners' notes

Using these concepts accurately and effectively can help to demonstrate your evaluative skills on the methods questions on this paper.

## Evaluating sociological research

Sociological research can be evaluated by using the four key concepts of:

1 **validity**
2 **reliability**
3 **representativeness**
4 **generalizability**.

These concepts can be linked to various aspects of sociological research:

- the theoretical perspective that underpins the research
- whether the data is **quantitative** or **qualitative**
- how **access** was gained
- practical issues of money, time and location
- **value freedom**
- **objectivity**
- **ethics**.

### 1. Validity

Validity is the extent to which the data is a true picture of the social reality of those being studied so that the research does what it set out to do. Validity is particularly important to interpretative sociologists who seek to find the meanings and motives people attach to their actions and the actions of others. They collect qualitative data that is rich and detailed.

## Examiners' notes

Use studies to support your points. You can be time effective in revision if you understand in some detail studies that can be used to support a range of arguments. You will also have more confidence in using these studies.

In order to obtain this type of data the researcher needs to be able to have a **rapport** with the group or individuals they are researching, so that they gain **verstehen**. They also want to be able to probe the responses people give.

MacDonald and Marsh spent a long time with the youths they researched in Teesside, as did Craine with those he researched in Manchester. Both studies were **ethnographic**, combining **observation** with **unstructured interviews** and some group discussions. This allowed them to get to know the youths in detail and, as far as it is possible for researchers who are studying the lives of the young and **disconnected**, to understand what it was like to be those youths.

Critics of this type of research argue that there is a chance the researcher will **'go native'**. They are also likely to operationalize key terms in a partial and subjective way and impose their values on the research, particularly when they write it up. For example, MacDonald and Marsh prefaced their analysis with a sustained argument against the New Right view of the **underclass**.

## Essential notes

MacDonald and Marsh could respond to critics by arguing that this gave their research added validity by making it clear what they were setting out to do–that is, challenge the New Right theory of the underclass in relation to youth.

### 2. Reliability

Reliability is the extent to which the research can be replicated by the same sociologist at another time, or by a different sociologist, and the same or similar results be obtained. Factors relating to the reliability of data include:

- The extent to which the sampling technique is transparent. It would be difficult to replicate research where the type of sample is very different from the original.
- Whether the measuring instrument is standardized. For example, when a questionnaire is used everyone should be asked the same questions in the same order.

- The way questions in a **structured interview** are asked. They must be asked in the same way as well as the same order, so that any variation between respondents is not because of the interviewer.

Reliability is important to **positivists** who want to identify **patterns** and **trends**, find correlations or make comparisons with other groups or over a period of time. For example, the Hills Report identified patterns of inequality and trends over time. It was based on secondary data from a number of large-scale government surveys, such as the Labour Force Survey and Family Resources Survey. The sources could easily be checked by others and the original surveys were based on standardized questionnaires.

Positivists argue that research must be carried out logically and systematically in an unbiased and objective way.

Critics, however, argue that no research is entirely value free (see page 68) since even structured questionnaires are socially constructed, with the researcher deciding what to ask and what to omit.

## 3. Representativeness
Representativeness is the extent to which the sample being researched are a fair reflection of the target population and are typical of those in the target population.

Positivist sociologists are particularly keen to obtain a representative sample so they can generalize from the findings of the research to the target population.

To obtain a representative sample researchers need to use a **random sampling** technique such as **stratified random sampling** and ensure they avoid having a skewed sample.

A good example of representative research is the ELSA study (see page 35) which recruited respondents using a sampling method that would provide a 'representative sample of the English population aged 50 and over'. The study was based on 12 000 respondents.

## 4. Generalizability
Generalizability is the extent to which it is safe to apply the findings from the research to the **target population**. In order to do this the sample needs to be both large enough and typical of the target population.

Positivists seek to make generalizations, but interpretivists are less concerned about this because they want to obtain an insight into the lives of those they study. For example, Bhopal's research provided an insight into the working experiences and home life of the women she studied.

## Ethics
The BSA has guidelines that they recommend all researchers follow. However, some ethnographers, such as Patrick, argue that to do so would be to reduce or destroy their chances of gaining an insight into the lives of the groups they are studying. (See pages 70–71 for more detail on ethical issues.)

**Essential notes**

Skewed samples are those that only partially reflect the target population, often as a result of using too small a sample.

**Essential notes**

It can be argued that the findings of some small studies might be true of other people in the same situation. For example, Archer's study on university aspirations was based on schools in London, but young working-class students in other parts of the country might also feel university is not for them because they consider they are, like their London counterparts, more 'a Nike person'.

## Questionnaires

Questionnaires are one way of carrying out a **social survey**. They are often used by **positivists** because this allows them to collect large amounts of quantitative data in a logical and scientific way that can be considered to be **objective.**

A questionnaire is a set of standardized questions, distributed by hand, mail or the internet. They are designed for self-completion and everyone is asked the same questions in the same order.

### Designing a questionnaire

Factors to be taken into account when designing questionnaires are:

- The aim of the research needs to be clear so that questions collect the data required.
- The need for consistency in the use of terms. The meaning should be the same for everyone.
- Designers should create clearly worded questions which are not ambiguous, do not lead the respondent into a response and are not 'double-barrelled' (two or three questions in one).
- The need to avoid technical language.

### Types of questions

There are three basic types of questions:

- Closed – responses are pre-set.
- Open – tend to ask how people feel about something, or why they did something.
- Attitudinal scale – ask respondents to rank their answers on a numerical or rating scale. Here the critical issue is the problem of phrases such as strongly agree/disagree when the meaning of 'strong' will vary from person to person.

### Pilot studies

Pilot studies are often used when designing questionnaire research. They allow the researcher to identify and resolve potential problems regarding:

- the sample and access
- the method of distribution
- the wording of the questions
- the layout of the questionnaire
- the language used
- the extent to which the data obtained is what is required.

The researcher can ask those who took part for feedback as another way to 'iron out' problems. The pilot study saves time and money by sorting out problems before the main survey is conducted and can sometimes even help refine the research objectives.

### Advantages and disadvantages of questionnaires

Some advantages and disadvantages apply to all questionnaires, and some are more specifically relevant to questionnaires that are mailed or sent via the internet.

| | Advantages | Disadvantages |
|---|---|---|
| **Questionnaires in general** | • Relatively cheap, quick and easy<br>• Completed by the respondents themselves, little involvement of the researcher<br>• People can complete in their own time<br>• Anonymous, so people may be prepared to divulge sensitive material they would not in face-to-face situations – this will increase validity<br>• Avoids the 'interviewer effect'<br>• Can be translated (Nazroo points out the usefulness of this)<br>• Can be replicated<br>• Likely the same or similar results will be obtained, data therefore likely to be reliable<br>• Can be used in conjunction with other methods to provide a fuller picture<br>• Pre-coded responses are easy to analyse by computer<br>• Statistical data will allow for comparisons to be made and patterns and trends identified<br>• Can establish **causal links**<br>• No danger to the researchers | • Questionnaires are **socially constructed** and reflect the values and interests of the researcher<br>• Sample may end up skewed if the response rate is low. May mean results are not **representative** of the target population and it is therefore unsafe to make **generalizations**<br>• Respondent cannot ask for a question to be explained or expand on their response<br>• Researcher unable to dig deep; often what someone says they do differs from the reality of what they actually do – so data is likely to be low on validity |
| **Mailed questionnaires** | • Can be distributed across a wide geographic area (e.g. the British Household Panel Survey collects data from 5 500 households, or 10 300 individuals, from 250 areas of the UK) | • Needs carefully worded cover letter explaining the purpose of the questionnaire and guaranteeing anonymity and confidentiality<br>• Researcher can never be sure who has completed it<br>• Response rate is often low – 40% is considered to be reasonable but it can be much less<br>• Respondents may be a self-selected group, not typical of the target population |

**Table 2**
Questionnaires: advantages and disadvantages

**Examiners' notes**

Many of the same advantages and disadvantages apply to questionnaires posted on the internet as those that are mailed. However, remember that not everyone has the internet and many people may be wary of responding to an online questionnaire.

## Interviews

There are four main types of interviews:

1 structured
2 unstructured
3 semi-structured
4 group, including focus groups.

This type of research is usually conducted face-to-face, but the first three can be done over the telephone.

The table below shows the relationship between method, the type of data obtained and the theoretical perspective that supports each approach.

**Table 3**
Types of interview

**Examiners' notes**

Ensure you understand the links between theory and method.

| Type of interview | Type of data gathered | Perspective |
|---|---|---|
| Structured | Quantitative | Positivist |
| Unstructured | Qualitative | Interpretivist/feminist |
| Semi-structured | Quantitative and qualitative | No particular perspective |
| Group/Focus group | Qualitative | Interpretivist/feminist |

Unstructured interviews are used by **interpretivists**, who want to find out about the experiences of the people they are researching and the meanings they attach to their actions. This approach is also preferred by **feminists**, who want to minimize the **hierarchical relationship** between the researcher and the interviewee and empower them as far as possible. **Positivists** prefer to use a more structured and 'scientific' approach.

### 1. Structured interviews

A structured interview involves a set of pre-determined questions. The questions are closed, although occasionally there is a 'catch all' open question at the end where interviewees are asked if they have anything else they wish to say.

**Essential notes**

In a structured interview, as opposed to a questionnaire, the interviewer writes down the responses rather than the respondent.

| Advantages | Disadvantages |
|---|---|
| • Interviewer has control<br>• Questions and procedures are pre-determined<br>• All interviewees asked the same questions in the same order<br>• Interviewer may be permitted to explain a question if the interviewee is unclear. This is not always allowed<br>• Face-to-face interview allows researcher to see the body language of the interviewee<br>• Interview questions are standardized and therefore the research can be replicated | • **Interviewer effect** can occur (interviewee may change what they say as a result of the gender, age, perceived class or ethnicity of the interviewer)<br>• If there is a team of researchers, they may use different voice tones and body language (could also occur with the same interviewer)<br>• If more than one researcher is required, there will be a cost for training<br>• Time-consuming |

| Advantages | Disadvantages |
|---|---|
| • Data collected is likely to be reliable<br>• If the sample is selected systematically, it is possible to make comparisons with other groups, or the same group at a later date, or to identify patterns and/or trends<br>• If the sample is large enough and a fair reflection of the target population, generalizations can be made<br>• Answers are easy to record and analysis can be done by computer<br>• Can reduce the number of refusals (compared to questionnaires) | • Some interviewees may be put off by pre-coded questions and answers – the answer they want might not be provided, or they may have liked some different questions<br>• Opportunity to misinterpret the questions – will reduce validity<br>• Do not allow respondent to elaborate upon what they are saying so depth of information will be limited – will reduce validity<br>• Refusals may lead to a skewed sample |

**Table 4**
Structured interviews: advantages and disadvantages

## 2. Unstructured interviews

An unstructured interview is an open-ended, informal interview. The interviewer will know what they want to cover in terms of topics but will allow a 'conversation' to develop and give the interviewee some control of the situation.

| Advantages | Disadvantages |
|---|---|
| • Can develop a relationship with the interviewee based on trust – they may then reveal more information making the data more valid. (For this relationship to develop the interviewer needs good personal skills)<br>• Interviewer may achieve *verstehen* – an understanding of how the respondent feels<br>• Interviewer may develop a **rapport**, making communication more relaxed and increasing the possibility of valid data. (Gaining rapport particularly helps when the subject matter is sensitive or personal) | • Interviewer needs to keep the interviewee focused without disrupting their flow or imposing their own views on them<br>• Cannot be repeated; they are unique encounters, which means the data will be low in reliability<br>• 'Conversation' will be guided by the researcher<br>• Gender, class and ethnicity of the interviewer could lead to an interviewer effect (e.g. the South Asian women Bhopal interviewed could have been intimidated by her class and work status and perhaps not revealed aspects of their lives they thought she might not approve of). If that happens, validity will be reduced |

### Essential notes

Hobson (1998) argues that informal and unstructured interviews are not the same thing: informality is about the relationship between the interviewer and the interviewee, whereas unstructured refers to the extent to which questions are pre-set.

☞ This topic continues on the next two pages

| Advantages | Disadvantages |
|---|---|
| • Gaining a relationship with interviewees means they are more likely to attend at agreed times. (McDowell found if the young men she was studying forgot an appointment she could ring and they would usually come immediately)<br>• Interviewee can ask for clarification<br>• Interviewer can probe for more detailed information, perhaps something they would not have thought of asking about<br>• Interviewer may obtain data not possible to acquire in other ways about people's feelings, for example, on domestic violence<br>• Interviewer can sometimes learn about related issues from the interviewee<br>• Once a rapport has been developed and a relationship of trust secured, the researcher can go back to interviewees after data has been analysed to check they are portraying what has been said accurately | • Sample size is usually small. This means the sample may not be representative (e.g. Hauari and Hollingworth's study on fathering took place in materially deprived inner-city areas in London, the Midlands and the North West. Families in materially deprived rural areas, for example, in Cornwall, were not included)<br>• If the sample is not representative then it is not safe to make generalizations<br>• Volume of data collected takes a long time to analyse<br>• Risk at the analysis stage that **researcher imposition** will occur (i.e. the views and values of the researcher determine the data they choose to use) |

## Examiners' notes

Accurate use of concepts such as researcher imposition will demonstrate your sociological understanding of methodology.

## Essential notes

When researchers ask respondents to check what they have written it is known as **respondent validation**.

**Table 5**
Unstructured interviews: advantages and disadvantages

## Key study

### Hauari and Hollingworth: Understanding fathering

Fathering and the changing role of what men do and are expected to do is a sensitive subject and unstructured interviews are more likely to provide a deep, rich understanding of the current views of some parents.

Hauari and Hollingworth's study was based on 29 two-parent families. The sample comprised 10 Pakistani families, 10 white, seven black Caribbean and two black African, all of whom came from inner-city areas with high deprivation. The children ranged from seven to 18 years old. Unstructured interviews conducted in the homes of the respondents were used as a means of collecting qualitative data on the changing nature of fatherhood. The research found some variation between the views of the different ethnic groups, but found all of the fathers were wanting or expecting to play a greater role in the lives of their children and were pleased to be doing so.

**Source:** Hauari, H. and Hollingworth, K. *Understanding Fathering: Masculinity, Diversity and Change* (Joseph Rowntree Foundation, 2009)

## 3. Group interviews and focus groups

A group interview may be quite wide-ranging, as with Frosh's study of young masculinities, whereas a focus group is usually concerned with a specific topic.

| Advantages | Disadvantages |
|---|---|
| • More people can be involved<br>• Members of the group can bounce ideas off each other<br>• Groups empower people<br>• Researchers can obtain in-depth information<br>• Participants can reflect and rethink what they say, potentially making the data more valid | • Can be difficult to record<br>• Dominant participants may 'take over'<br>• Interviewer effect can occur<br>• Participants may say what they think the researcher (or their peers) wants to hear |

**Essential notes**

In a group interview, the researcher may interject questions and ensure the discussion keeps going. In a focus group, the group members have more of a discussion with each other.

**Table 6**
Group interviews: advantages and disadvantages

### Key study

**Frosh et al.: Young masculinities**

The researchers wanted to gain an insight into young masculinities. Group interviews took place in 12 London schools with 245 boys, 11–14 years old, and 27 girls. There were 45 group interviews with between four and eight young people in each, 36 groups were boys only, nine were mixed. What was discussed in the groups depended on who was in them, but the researcher had a list of topic headings in case the group had not covered areas the researchers thought might be interesting.

**Essential notes**

Feminists argue group interviews reduce the hierarchical relationship between the researcher and those being researched.

**Source:** Frosh, S. et al. *Young Masculinities* (Palgrave, 2002)

## 4. Semi-structured interviews

Semi-structured interviews obtain both **qualitative** and **quantitative** data. They are often used when researchers wish to maximize the advantages of structured and unstructured interviews and minimize their disadvantages.

### Key study

**Pope: Out in the field**

Pope decided to use semi-structured interviews in order to combine a positivist approach with an interpretivist one.

Pope's research was an opportunity to find out about the backgrounds and experiences of female football fans. She built a rapport with her respondents because she was young, female and a football supporter. Using semi-structured interviews enabled her 'to stay in control'. She also chose the method in order to be able to draw comparisons between respondents as well as enabling them to expand on their answers.

**Source:** Pope, S. *Out in the Field Sociology Review* 17:4 (Philip Allan, 2008)

**Essential notes**

When observation is combined with unstructured interviews the research is often described as **ethnographic**.

## Observation

Observation is carried out in the natural environment of those being studied. This type of research is usually used by interpretive sociologists who want to collect qualitative data from the point of view of those they are studying. By using an observation schedule or matrix it is also possible to collect quantitative data.

The researcher may take a role as a participant in the group or stay on the outside for non-participant observation.

A key variation with participant observation is whether the group knows they are being observed – **overt observation**; or is not aware, as is the case when the sociologist either infiltrates the group or takes on an undercover role to enable the observation to take place – **covert observation**.

There are a number of advantages and disadvantages that apply to any type of observation and a few that are specific to the particular type.

**Essential notes**

The Hawthorne effect is where those who are being studied behave differently as a result of knowing they are being researched.

| Advantages | Disadvantages |
|---|---|
| • Researcher may observe the group in their natural environment and gain detailed, rich data about them<br>• May gain an insight into the group and the meanings they attach to their activities<br>• May obtain valid data as a result of the depth of the data<br>• May gain ideas for further research by observing and being involved with a group (Whyte said he gained answers to questions he would not have thought of asking) | • Need to gain access could take time; some sociologists gain access through a person already involved in the group or by an introduction from a 'gatekeeper' (Blackman gained access to the New Wave Girls through the Mod boys, one of whom had a girlfriend in the group)<br>• Time and place of the observation will be fixed<br>• Research may take a long time and costs may therefore be high<br>• Researcher may get too involved and lose the ability to stand back<br>• The **Hawthorne effect** may occur<br>• Reliability of the data will be low since it is very difficult to repeat observations<br>• Researcher imposition may occur when the data is analysed<br>• Sample will not necessarily be representative or typical of anyone but themselves<br>• Generalization will be unsafe |

**Table 7**
General advantages and disadvantages of observation

### Participant observation

In order to carry out participant observation, the social characteristics of the researcher (gender, age, ethnicity and class) need to be close to those of the group, especially if the observation is to be covert.

Potential ethical issues also need to be considered. The researcher Hobbs decided to be involved with illegal activities in order to maintain his insider status with some of the groups in the East End.

The question of how involved to get and for how long then needs to be thought through. The longer the involvement, the more likely the researcher is to either '**go native**' or influence the behaviour of the group.

Whyte affected the street corner society he studied. They knew he was there and Doc, the leader, said 'You've slowed me down plenty, I have to think what Bill Whyte would want to know and think how I could explain it. Before I just used to do things.'

There are some advantages and disadvantages that are specific to each type of observation.

| | Advantages | Disadvantages |
|---|---|---|
| **Overt participant observation** | • Researcher will be able to ask questions when appropriate (Barker did this when she studied the religious sect known as the Moonies) | • Hawthorne effect may change the behaviour of the group. (Willis argued that after a while the lads got used to him and carried on more or less as usual; any changes were simply an exaggeration of how they were when he was not there. However, it is arguable whether the same could be said for Blackman's research with the New Wave Girls. They may well have acted differently with a young male hanging around with them.) |
| **Covert participant observation** | • Avoids suspicion by the group if it is engaged in illegal activities<br>• Data will be valid because the group will treat the researcher as one of them<br>• Hawthorne effect will be minimalized<br>• Can gain *verstehen*<br>• Can develop a rapport with the members of the group | • Risk of going native<br>• Little if any chance of repeating the research, therefore reliability is low<br>• Getting out may be problematic<br>• Researcher will be unable to get informed consent<br>• It is unethical and may place the researcher in danger<br>• Recording field notes will be a problem |
| **Overt non-participant observation** | • Consent can be obtained | • Lack of involvement may mean the researcher misunderstands what is happening |

**Table 8**
Overt and covert observation: advantages and disadvantages

## Structured observation

This is a systematic observation which generates quantitative data and is usually used when the researcher knows what they are looking for and wants to record the frequency of what is being studied.

## Content analysis

Content analysis is a method of collecting quantitative and qualitative data. It is primarily used to analyse the mass media and historical documents.

### Types of content analysis

#### 1. Formal content analysis

This is a statistical exercise in which previously identified categories are counted and 'ticked off' on a pre-coded grid.

- Best used this strategy to examine the **sex roles** in pre-school children's books.

#### 2. Thematic analysis

With this approach, an area of reporting is identified and the number of times the theme appears is counted.

**Essential notes**

Beharrell's research with the GUMG looked at coverage of HIV/AIDS over a period of nearly three years.

- Beharrell used thematic content analysis in his study of HIV/AIDS coverage in newspapers. He was able to identify the different type of coverage of the tabloid press compared to the broadsheets and suggests this reflected the biases of the different types of papers at the time.
- Pawson also argues it is sometimes used to uncover the ideological biases of journalists.

#### 3. Textual analysis

This approach involves a textual analysis in terms of the use of language that leads readers into particular interpretations of news and stories. It has similarities to **semiology**, which analyses signs and symbols in order to decode and understand the messages contained in the text.

- The Glasgow University Media Group (GUMG), under the direction of Greg Philo, have used this approach in a number of their studies on news reporting. For example, their analysis of the 1976 strike at the car plant at Longbridge highlighted the different adjectives and descriptive words used about the strikers compared to the management.

### Key study

#### Wayne et al.: Television news and young people

One strand of the research by Wayne et al. about the relationship between television news, politics and young people was to analyse 2000 television news reports on all channels, including Sky News, for one month in 2006. They were interested in how often young people were either used as news sources, or were significant 'actors' in the stories. They found 286 stories which featured young people as the main focus. Of these, 69% were about crime and most of the remainder were about young celebrities, particularly footballers. As with the GUMG's research on HIV/AIDS, they also used focus groups as a further strand of their research.

**Source:** Wayne, M. *Television News and Young People, Sociology Review*, 19(1) (Philip Allan, 2009)

## 4. Audience analysis

This is a way of finding out the audience response to media content. It enables the researcher to check their own interpretations against those of the audience. Doing this overcomes the criticism of the other three approaches that the audience are passive recipients of media messages. The GUMG have used focus groups in some of their research to gain the audience perspective. For example, the research on HIV/AIDS undertook quantitative and qualitative content analysis and 52 focus groups with 351 individuals were held.

## Research design decisions

There are a number of decisions that need to be made specific to content analysis. Once the researcher has decided what strategy of the above four to use, they need to choose what media to include. They should be careful that this does not simply reflect the values of the researcher.

If formal content analysis is to be used, the research question must be clearly defined to ensure that the coding schedule does not miss relevant categories. Once identified, these categories need to be formally set out.

As with all types of research, there are specific advantages and disadvantages.

**Examiners' notes**

Ensure you understand the difference between these four types of content analysis and, in particular, the difference between formal content analysis which collects quantitative data and textual analysis which collects qualitative data.

| Advantages | Disadvantages |
|---|---|
| • It is cheap; news coverage can be accessed at little or no cost from TV broadcasts, the internet and newspapers<br>• Sources are easily available<br>• Allows researchers to make comparisons. By quantifying results, they can compare news reporting or representation across channels, newspapers, media, over time and between societies<br>• The coding system can be applied by anyone. This means it can be repeated and, if quantitative data is being collected on a pre-coded grid, the same or similar results will probably be found – making it reliable<br>• More than one of the approaches can be used in order to check the validity of the data collected<br>• Can also be used with other methods (e.g. in his research on the media and mental illness, Philo conducted a content analysis over a period of one month of press and TV news plus popular magazines and popular TV. Focus groups were also used) | • Coding categories are **socially constructed**; they are **subjective** so may be affected by the researcher's political biases which will influence findings<br>• Possible to misinterpret the meaning<br>• Problem of understanding what messages readers are receiving from a text<br>• Formal content analysis on its own reveals nothing about meanings – merely counts how often something appears in a programme<br>• Semiological analysis is entirely subjective and therefore very low in reliability |

**Table 9**
Content analysis: advantages and disadvantages

## Secondary data

Secondary data are data that have been collected or created by someone else for their own purposes, but which the sociologist can then use. There are three main sources:

- quantitative data such as official statistics
- public and personal documents
- the internet.

### Official statistics

Official statistics are generally derived from compulsory registrations, such as births and deaths, or large-scale government surveys such as the Labour Force Survey. These surveys cover all aspects of social life including education, employment, crime and health.

**Positivists** use official statistics because they provide 'hard' data. They argue that statistics are reliable because the research can be repeated and the same results found.

### Essential notes

The data from government surveys is often published in *Social Trends* or on the Office for National Statistics (ONS) website.

### Examiners' notes

Keep up-to-date by going to the websites on a regular basis and also reading *Social Trends*, which includes commentaries as well as the tables and graphs.

### Essential notes

Data on poverty are based on a government definition of poverty which differs from the various definitions used by sociologists.

### Essential notes

Some government surveys use **semi-structured interviews** which provide more detail and therefore increase validity.

| Advantages | Disadvantages |
|---|---|
| • Easy to access, from free government websites<br>• Up-to-date, many are collected annually or biennially<br>• Frequency of collection enables comparisons to be made year on year<br>• Comparisons can be made between social groups (e.g. HESA data on the social class of students entering university)<br>• Patterns and trends can be identified<br>• The effect of legislation can be tracked (e.g. effect of increasing student fees on numbers applying to university)<br>• Usually based on standardized measuring instruments such as questionnaires, therefore can be replicated<br>• Sample size is usually large, making it likely the sample will be representative, which means it is possible to make generalizations<br>• Often used as a starting point for social research (Arber et al. studied the social lives of older men and started by analysing data from three large government surveys including the General Household Survey and the British Household Panel Survey)<br>• Can be used to inform or support social policies such as health initiatives<br>• Can allow a sociologist to reach groups whom they might not otherwise have access to<br>• Can be used to test a **hypothesis** (Durkheim did this with his study of suicide)<br>• Data can be analysed by sociologists in new ways (e.g. the Hills Report) | • Based on questionnaires designed by the government; consequently questions may not be those a sociologist would choose to ask<br>• Concepts have been operationalized by the government, so may reflect their priorities<br>• No chance to prompt and probe respondents so validity may be low<br>• Can be manipulated – data in some areas, such as employment and crime, can be collected in a way that makes the government appear in a better light<br>• Do not give a full picture (e.g. crime statistics only include reported crime) |

**Table 10**
Official statistics: advantages and disadvantages

## Public and personal documents

Public documents either come from government sources, for example, Ofsted reports or the Hills Report, or from pressure groups such as the Child Poverty Action Group.

Personal documents can come in many forms; they include diaries, letters, pictures, photos and audio recordings.

**Examiners' notes**

These are sometimes referred to as **expressive documents** and provide qualitative data.

| Advantages | Disadvantages |
|---|---|
| • Usually cheap<br>• Easy to use<br>• Accessible<br>• Authentic true accounts, so high in validity (e.g. material from the Mass Observation Study has provided a rich and detailed source of people's lives since 1937)<br>• Provide detailed material, giving an insight into the lives of the people who created them<br>• Historical documents are able to provide material that would not otherwise be available to sociologists<br>• Can be checked by other researchers because they already exist in written, visual or audio form<br>• Sociologists sometimes ask the people they are researching to keep diaries or make drawings (e.g. Archer's study of Muslim boys included asking eight of them to keep photographic diaries) | • Many are one-off, (e.g. diaries) so there is nothing to cross check them against<br>• Lack representativeness (e.g. a historical diary will have been written by someone who was literate, which was not typical of their time)<br>• Interpretation of documents is subjective, particularly if the written meaning is unclear<br>• Material may be partial – simply the view of the individual writer<br>• Writers may not be typical of other people<br>• Lack reliability – cannot be repeated |

**Table 11**
Public and personal documents: advantages and disadvantages

**Essential notes**

The Mass Observation Survey collects data from 2000 people from a cross-section of the population on all aspects of 'the everyday lives of ordinary people'.

In considering documents, Scott suggested four criteria should be used:

1 Authenticity – whether a document is written by the person it says it is. Is it genuine?
2 Credibility – whether the documents are free from error or whether they are subject to the biases and distortions of the authors. For example, the political memoirs of politicians Tony Blair and Gordon Brown may offer very different interpretations of the same events.
3 Representativeness – the extent to which documents have survived and are accessible. Also if they are typical of the particular documents being used.
4 Meaning – the ability of the researcher to interpret the document.

## Essential notes

The debate as to the best source of 'true' knowledge is known as the epistemological debate: the debate about the nature of what constitutes knowledge.

## Essential notes

Some feminists are now adopting a mixed methods approach, collecting quantitative data as well as qualitative. (See pp 78–79 on feminism.)

## Essential notes

Denzin argues that validity can also be enhanced by the use of investigator triangulation – the use of more than one researcher to counter researcher bias. However, this is not always possible, especially with ethnographic research.

## Essential notes

Bryman argues that quantitative and qualitative methods are rarely 'tapping the same things' even when they appear to be investigating the same research issue.

**Table 12**
Triangulation: advantages and disadvantages

# Mixed methods research

**Positivists** and **interpretivists** have different views as to the best type of data to collect – quantitative or qualitative – but different methods are based on different sets of assumptions and there is no one method that can be said to be the most advantageous in identifying the 'truth'. In practice, using a mixed methods approach is quite common.

Mixed methods, multi-methods or multi-strategy research is used to improve the quality and validity of the data. According to Bryman (2001), this includes:

- facilitation
- **triangulation**
- **methodological pluralism** or a complementarity approach.

## Facilitation

This is the use of a method at the start of research to help formulate the research question or **hypothesis** which the rest of the research will then be based on.

## Triangulation

Triangulation is the use of more than one method, usually one or more that collects quantitative data and one or more that collects qualitative data, to:

- cross check the data being collected for accuracy (for example, using in-depth interviews to cross check the data from a large survey, as Dench et al. did in their study of East London)
- re-examine the data
- cross check the data for consistency
- counter the bias of the data of a single method
- increase confidence in the findings.

Although the use of two or more methods is normally planned, there are times when it might happen more naturally.

- The Newsons researched the patterns of infant care in the 1960s by interviewing 700 mothers of young babies in their homes in Nottingham. They were able to observe the way the mothers responded to their older children as well as what they said about their views on discipline. These did not always correlate. Some said they did not agree with smacking, yet during the interview did smack one of their older children.

| Advantages | Disadvantages |
|---|---|
| • Increases accuracy of the research data<br>• Improves validity (if someone has been economical with the truth or even lied in response to a question, an unstructured observation or interview can reveal what they really think) | • Assumes there is a 'truth' to be found<br>• Different results could emerge from the different methods being used<br>• Researchers may interpret results of the methods used in different ways<br>• Even if the combination of methods being used seem to come to similar conclusions, another method could uncover different findings |

## Methodological pluralism

Methodological pluralism refers to a mixed methods approach where methods (again, usually qualitative and quantitative) are combined to provide a fuller and more detailed picture of the topic under investigation. Often one method is used first and the results of this inform the way other methods are used. It is a strategy often used by realists who want to study different aspects of the research question.

| Advantages | Disadvantages |
|---|---|
| • Can provide a fuller, more detailed picture<br>• Each method produces a 'different slice of reality' (Denzin), therefore using a variety of methods can allow for a wider range of issues to be addressed<br>• Advantages and disadvantages of the methods used can counter-balance each other (Dench et al. started with secondary data from mostly official sources but went on to end their research with unstructured interviews)<br>• Possible to identify from a questionnaire who to follow up with an interview<br>• Qualitative methods can help to explain the broader picture captured by quantitative data<br>• Qualitative data can provide an examination of the small-scale phenomena that lie beneath the large-scale ones identified by macro quantitative data collection<br>• Bryman argues the use of mixed methods can control the extent to which the research is 'filtered' through the particular theoretical perspective of the researcher | • Collecting and analysing data can be time consuming<br>• Analysis can be quite complex<br>• Lack of depth as individual methods may not be fully explored |

**Table 13**
Methodological pluralism: advantages and disadvantages

### Key study

#### Dench et al. : The New East End

The research by Dench et al. took place in Bethnal Green 40 years after the classic study *Family and Kinship in East London* by Young and Willmott. The study used a multi-methods approach: they started by collating facts and figures on the area from already existing reports; then carried out a survey using structured interviews; 51 of the survey respondents were interviewed in-depth, sometimes more than once; they also interviewed local teachers, youth workers, council officials and long-standing residents, and finally in-depth interviews were carried out with young, mostly female, Bangladeshis. The interviews with all these groups after the survey enabled them to 'flesh out the survey findings and make better sense of them'.

**Source:** Dench et al. *The New East End: Kinship, Race and Conflict* (Profile Books, 2006)

**Essential notes**

Ritchie argues in a study on homelessness that quantitative data could provide a picture of different types of homelessness and the characteristics of the homeless, whilst the qualitative data would be able to uncover the experience of being homeless.

**Examiners' notes**

Students often use triangulation and methodological pluralism interchangeably – this demonstrates a lack of clarity and precision, so think carefully about the differences between them.

## Sampling

Sampling is the selection of a group to study from the target, or survey, population. When quantitative data is being collected a sample should be chosen on the basis of being **representative** of the target population. A large representative sample will mean the findings of the research will be able to be **generalized**.

The ten-yearly census carried out for the government by the Office for National Statistics is based on the UK population as a whole. It is carried out in the first year of each decade. All other research involves the sociologist choosing a sample of individuals or social groups they want to use for their research.

Various factors need to be considered by the researcher when selecting a sample. These include:

- Identification of the target population.
- Identifying what **sampling frames**, if any, are available.
- Finding how to access the sampling frame and/or the target population.
- Understanding who is included in the sampling units.
- Deciding what size the sample should be.
- Working out what sampling strategy to use.

### Sampling frames

A sampling frame is a list of the target population. For example:

- The Electoral Register – a list of all those eligible to vote in the UK.
- The Postcode Address File (PAF) – this includes all UK households in each postcode.
- School or university registers.
- Payroll list – includes all employees of a company.

There can be problems associated with sampling frames. These include:

- They may be out of date. For example, when people move it may take them a while to update their address details.
- They may not include everyone in the target population. For example, not all school-aged children will be on a school register as the home-schooled, traveller children and the long-term hospitalized are not included.
- They may not identify ethnicity, gender or age.
- Many files may not be available for confidentiality reasons.
- There are no lists of groups such as the homeless.

In order to access sampling frames, a **gatekeeper** is sometimes required. This is someone like a head teacher who controls access to the sampling frame, in this case, the school register of all students.

### Sampling techniques

Sampling techniques can broadly be divided into two types:

1. Random or probability sampling. This means everyone in the target population has the same chance, or probability, of being selected. It is seen as objective and scientific. This is used by positivists who want a representative sample.

2 Non-random sampling. This is more likely to be used by interpretivists who are more interested in finding specific types of individuals or groups than ensuring that their target is statistically representative.

## Random or probability sampling

Simple random sampling involves selecting a certain number of entries from a list, usually one that is computer generated. Systematic random sampling involves the selection of every *n*th name or unit from a list. Stratified random sampling is the technique favoured by researchers who want to ensure they obtain a truly representative sample. The target population is divided into the social characteristics the researcher is interested in, such as gender, age or ethnicity. The sample is then randomly selected from a list for each category. The sample should then be a fair reflection of the target population – it should be representative.

## Cluster sampling

The target population is sub-divided, then a random sample is selected from the sub-divisions, then a further sample from those samples and so on, until a final sample of the required size is achieved

## Non-random sampling

Quota sampling: this is a useful method if the demographics of the target population are known. People are selected by the researcher according to the categories they fit into, and the number required from each category

Purposeful sampling: this technique is used when a certain sample profile is required (e.g. Jackson in her study on lads and ladettes selected her schools carefully to ensure a mix of pupils in terms of social class, race and ethnicity).

Snowball sampling: this technique is often used when a group is difficult to access. It involves a contact introducing the researcher to other people (e.g. Devine used it as a means of contacting doctors for her Manchester sample).

Opportunity sampling: involves the researcher asking people who happen to be about and 'fit' the criteria to take part (e.g. stopping people in the street to complete a survey).

Volunteer sampling: often involves advertising for people who fit certain criteria to get in touch (e.g. a notice in local newspapers).

## Evaluation of random sampling

Random sampling techniques can be repeated and a similar group will probably emerge; this makes it a reliable method of selecting a sample. Additionally, if the sample is large enough it is likely to be representative and therefore it will be safe to generalize.

However, selecting representative samples is time-consuming and if the sampling frame fails to provide relevant information such as age or ethnicity, stratified sampling is not possible. This means that sometimes skewed or biased samples may be produced.

## Evaluation of non-random sampling

This methodology is useful when there is no sampling frame or when a specific type of person or group is required, or a group is difficult to reach.

However, samples are unlikely to be representative. Even when selecting a quota sample, the researcher may be swayed by their impressions of people.

## Essential notes

If the target population is all schools in an area it would be economical of time and money to use a cluster sample of three areas within the main area, and then either use all the schools in those areas or do another random sample to select just some of them.

## Essential notes

Devine was attempting to reach people she might have otherwise found difficult to reach. She was collecting qualitative data to gain an insight into the lives of those she was studying and did not need a representative sample.

## Essential notes

Researchers who are doing ethnographic studies sometimes use more than one technique. For example, Bhopal used personal contact, advertising and a snowball strategy.

## Longitudinal studies

A longitudinal study is carried out over a period of years in order to study changes or developments over time. It can also be used to identify **causal relationships** and **correlations** between, say, health and class.

Longitudinal studies may take various forms, including panel studies and cohort studies.

### Panel studies

The data is collected from a sample selected from sampling frames such as the Postcode Address File. The sample unit may be individuals, households or organizations.

An example of a panel survey is the British Household Panel Study (BHPS). This was first carried out in 1991 with a representative sample of 5 500 households who were selected from the national Postcode Address File. The BHPS is carried out annually. All members of the households selected were interviewed in the first year and then re-interviewed in each subsequent year. Any members of the households who have moved away are also contacted and re-interviewed, together with members of their new households.

### Cohort studies

A **cohort study** is one based on people with the same social characteristic, often their age. It may be a whole group, such as a class in a school, or a sample of the group.

The first cohort study, the National Survey of Health and Development, was carried out on all babies born in the first week of March 1946. J.W.B. Douglas et al. (1964, 1970) used the same cohort of 5 362 children to study the relationship between class and **educational achievement**.

### Methods used to collect longitudinal data

The data for longitudinal studies is usually collected by questionnaires or interviews, although some researchers such as Skeggs have used ethnographic methods. Skeggs (1991, 1997) studied 83 working-class mothers over a period of 12 years, during which she was in continual contact with them.

Many longitudinal studies use a mixed methods approach to data collection. The English Longitudinal Study of Ageing (ELSA), which was started in 2002, collects data via interviews, questionnaires and visits to the respondents by nurses.

Some **participant observation** studies take three or four years and could therefore be described as longitudinal studies.

### Decisions about the research design

The cost of the research and analysis of a longitudinal study is inevitably high. This means that the selection of the initial sample is extremely important and often involves a number of complicated stages.

A decision about how long the research will be financed for also needs to be made, as well as how often the data should be collected. The National

Child Development Study (NCDS), set up in 1958 to study all babies born in a week in March, has contacted the sample eight times so far. The ELSA has contacted their sample four times and the BHPS contacts their sample annually.

In addition, a decision must be taken regarding what to do about **attrition**. Attrition refers to members of the sample dropping out of the research or becoming uncontactable. Gauntlett and Hill maintained a personal contact with their sample which helped to slow attrition down – they lost just 82 of their original 509, but the NCDS lost approximately 6000 of its original 17400.

| Advantages | Disadvantages |
|---|---|
| • Changes in opinions or attitudes can be tracked over time<br>• Correlations can be identified (such as the link between class and health, identified by the ELSA)<br>• Possible to make **comparisons** with data from other studies<br>• Data from a study can be used to inform policy making. (One of the aims of the ELSA is to help the government plan for a growing ageing population)<br>• The data can be quantitative or qualitative, or both<br>• In-depth data can be obtained – even though some studies are based on questionnaires, after a period of time the data becomes increasingly rich and detailed and validity is obtained<br>• A relationship of trust can be established as the respondents feel at ease with the researchers (even if the study is conducted by post) | • Time consuming and expensive to run and to analyse<br>• Access to an appropriate sample is sometimes problematic<br>• Attrition will occur – people die, drop out or simply move. This can lead to a distorted sample and skewed results. (The ELSA resolved this problem by adding people from the original population sampled. In fact, they added more than had dropped out in order to maintain appropriate numbers at the lower age range of their sample)<br>• If attrition of the sample is high representativeness may be lowered and generalizability will be unsafe<br>• Researchers could 'go native' or become too close to their sample. (This was a criticism levelled at Skeggs and the working-class women she studied)<br>• The Hawthorne effect can occur as respondents build a relationship with the researchers. They know what might be expected and either change their behaviour or answer as expected<br>• Attrition of researchers – people change their jobs or retire |

**Examiners' notes**

In a question on longitudinal studies, ensure you answer with specific reference to studies over periods of time and not surveys in general.

**Table 14**
Longitudinal studies: advantages and disadvantages

## Case studies

Case studies are detailed in-depth studies of a group, an individual, an organization, an incident, an event or indeed any single example of what the researcher wants to investigate. Case studies may stand alone or be part of a larger piece of research. One characteristic of a case study is that the individual, the group or the event maintains some individuality; they are not 'lost' as in a large research study.

Case studies use a variety of methods. Many are based on the collection of qualitative data such as observation or unstructured interviews, others use a combination of quantitative and qualitative data to gain as wide-ranging an insight as possible of the 'case' being studied.

| Advantages | Disadvantages |
| --- | --- |
| • Can act as a start to more wide-ranging research, allowing the researcher to gain an insight into the area being studied and obtain ideas for further research<br>• Might throw up facts that need further research<br>• Can be used to generate a hypothesis<br>• Provide an insight into a 'case' which others might find difficult to access (e.g. Blackman's study of the New Wave Girls)<br>• Provide an insight into 'deviant' groups who might not be included in a large-scale study<br>• Can be conducted by a single researcher. (Gaining access for more than one researcher would have been impossible in the case of the Glasgow street gang Patrick studied)<br>• Tend to be high in validity – range of methods used means data can be cross-checked and time spent with a group means in-depth data can be collected (Willis spent over a year with the 'lads')<br>• Researcher can develop a rapport with those they are studying (Whyte, in his case study of a street corner society, gained 'answers to questions he might not have thought of asking') | • Case studies focus on a particular group and do not claim to be representative; however, they can be used as a starting point for other research (McDowell refers back to Willis in her 21st century study of young men about to leave school)<br>• Even though case studies are unlikely to be based on a representative sample, the sample may be **typical** of others (Blackman's 'New Wave Girls' may be typical of girl groups)<br>• Since the sample is not representative it is not safe to make generalizations (Goldthorpe and Lockwood's approach was to identify a 'case' where something was expected and then when it was not found they argued that it could be safe to make a generalization – i.e. if car-workers who were being paid well and lived in good housing had not become embourgeoisiefied then it was also unlikely that other groups of affluent workers would have done so)<br>• Platt (1993) argues there is a danger that even experienced researchers begin to make generalized comments when it is not safe to do so |

| Advantages | Disadvantages |
|---|---|
| • Possible to gain *verstehen* – the researcher is likely to spend a long time with the individuals or groups and develop a sensitivity to their situation<br>• Where quantitative data is collected, reliability could be achievable<br>• Can be useful to do a case study within a large-scale piece of research (e.g. Townsend studied a few families in depth from his very large sample, giving an increased insight into the lives of the poor) | • Given the close relationship usually developed between the researcher and the researched it would be difficult to repeat the case study (although Stacey returned to Banbury 20 years after her first study of the town)<br>• Risk of the over-involvement of the researcher, of them 'going native'<br>• Problem of researcher imposition – this might be solved by **respondent validation** |

**Table 15**
Case studies: advantages and disadvantages

## Essential notes

Respondent validation is when the researcher checks with those being researched that what they have written is an accurate portrayal. Willis did this; however, the lads commented they understood the verbatim quotes from themselves but not Willis' interpretations.

## Key study

### Blackman: The youth 'underclass'

Blackman carried out a 'qualitative case study' of homeless young people in Brighton. He got to know the young people very well by becoming their 'drinking partner, friend, colleague and football player'. He realized that using a conventional interview technique would not give him the depth of data he wanted because the youth might be suspicious of interviews. Instead, he kept a field diary and at the end of the research period wrote it up as a series of narratives. The field diary would have included as much as possible of what he observed and the conversations he had with the youth. He wanted the narratives to 'allow a view into [the] personal and subjective world [of the youth]'.

## Examiners' notes

Ensure that you remain focused on case studies and do not drift into a general essay on the use of mixed methods or on collecting qualitative data.

**Source:** Blackman, S. *Destructing a Giro: A critical and ethnographic study of the youth 'underclass'* in MacDonald, R. (ed.) *Youth, the 'Underclass' and Social Exclusion* (Routledge, 1997)

## Values and sociological research

The debate between **positivism** and **interpretivism** – between whether sociology can or cannot be scientific – underpins the debate about values and **value freedom**; in other words, the extent to which sociology can be **objective**.

There are two main alternative positions.

### 1. Sociology can be value-free

Positivists argue that if sociology is to have credibility it must be objective and scientific; it must be value-free. Others argue that it is either not possible to ignore one's values or that it would be wrong to do so.

Many 19th century sociologists argued that objectivity was possible by following a scientific approach. Despite their differing views of society, Comte, Durkheim and Marx all believed that this was possible. Durkheim argued that social facts could be investigated and measured.

### Evaluation

The work of Marx, Durkheim and Weber was informed by their views of the world. For Marx this was that the **bourgeoisie** oppressed and exploited the **proletariat**, Durkheim had a view that inherited **wealth** should be abolished, and Weber argued that large bureaucracies were not helpful in terms of people's freedom and creativity.

Bowling (2004) argues it is 'naive to assume that [objectivity] is achieved in any field of research'.

### 2. All research is value-laden

Advocates of this position argue that values are present from the start of the research process.

For example, Gouldner contends that it is not possible to separate 'facts' from the values of the researcher and Mies argues that indifference to the researched should be replaced by 'conscious partiality'.

Values can be said to have an impact at each stage of the research process:

- **The initial idea**
  Researchers choose to research areas of social life of importance to them. Much of the work of MacDonald and his colleagues on Teesside is with marginalized, disconnected youth and Townsend spent most of his professional life researching poverty.
- **Choice of method**
  Interpretive sociologists argue that the structured questionnaires and interviews used by positivists are socially constructed and informed by the views and values of the researcher who decides which questions to ask and which to exclude. On the other hand, positivists argue that what an interpretivist observes during their research and what, of all the data they collect, they select to write about is informed by their values. This must, argue the positivists, affect the validity of the data collected, since no two researchers will 'see' the same.
- **Control of the research by a funding body**
  Gouldner argues that if someone is paying for the research, there will be a reason why they want it done. Philo agrees and says

**Essential notes**

These theorists were all working in the 19th century when the natural sciences were dominant and there was a focus on following an objective scientific approach to research.

**Essential notes**

This can be linked to the question of reliability versus validity.

that targeted funding is a way of silencing those voices which the dominant class would rather not be heard.

- **Career aspirations of the researcher**
  Gouldner argues that academics need to get published in order to develop their careers and therefore they may operate within the constraints of the dominant view.
- **Analysis of the results**
  This is a similar point to that made regarding the choice of method above. The issue is researcher imposition.
- **Publication of the results**
  The journal, publisher or organization willing to publish the results will tend to share the values of the researcher.

## Evaluation
Even those who argue that research is value-laden point out it is possible to be honest and transparent about the views of the researchers. Gouldner argued this was vital if research was to have credibility.

**Reflexivity** is a key factor. This relates to the willingness of the researcher to consider the implications of the methods they are using, the extent to which their values are affecting the research and what implications the research might be having on those being researched. Feminists are particularly concerned that this should be the case, and the work of Skeggs and McDowell illustrates their commitment to reflexivity.

Weber acknowledged the initial idea might be based on the values of the researcher but argred that thereafter it is possible to carry out the research in an **objective** and **value-free** manner. He argued that the initial idea would probably have 'value relevance'.

It is also possible to use a **narrative** approach whereby those being researched can have their voices heard without being dominated by the researcher. Oakley tried this in *From Here to Maternity*, as did McDowell in her study of working-class youths.

## Committed sociology
Committed sociologists argue that sociology should be more than academic research; it should attempt to change the world.

In 1967 Becker said, 'The question is not whether we should take sides, since we inevitably will, but rather whose side are we on?' Gouldner argued that the approach taken by Becker led to the study of the 'underdog' rather than those with **power** in society.

Feminists argue that research should empower the women being researched, whilst those working in the field of **race** and **race discrimination** argue that research should highlight the reality of **racism** for people and attempt to influence what is done about it.

## Evaluation
Committed sociology raises questions about ethics. Hobbs noted that he had to engage in illegal activities in order remain an 'insider'. Apart from illegal activities, there is the likelihood of over-involvement of the researcher with those they are researching – 'going native' – and potential collusion with unacceptable views.

**Examiners' notes**

Keep revising a range of concepts in order that you can use the language of sociology in the exam.

**Essential notes**

Consider ethics in conjunction with values and theoretical debates.

## Ethical issues

**Ethics** are concerned with the moral issues sociologists need to consider before embarking on research.

Sociologists frequently carry out research that is sensitive or intrusive. To protect the social groups and individuals being researched there are various codes of conduct. The British Sociological Association (BSA) publishes a Statement of Ethical Practice to guide its members. Universities and government bodies such as the NHS also have their own set of ethical guidelines.

Most codes of ethics will include, at a minimum, guidelines relating to informed consent, confidentiality and avoiding harm.

### Informed consent

The participants must be fully informed of the precise nature of the research and then willingly agree to take part. The participants should always be told what the research will be used for.

If the group or individuals being researched are under age, then parental consent is required. However, this could mean children are taking part in research when they might prefer not to.

**Essential notes**

The Hawthorne effect, or experimental effect, occurs when people are aware they are being researched and change their behaviour.

### Issues with informed consent

- When participants are fully informed, the Hawthorne effect may occur. This may affect the results of the research.
- It may be inappropriate to ask for informed consent if the research is ethnographic; for example, MacIntyre's undercover research on football hooligans.
- Teachers in the Rosenthal and Jacobson study were deceived, but the research could not have taken place had they been informed.
- Some groups, such as the elderly, are vulnerable and may agree to participate without realizing the full implications.
- It may not be possible to gain parental consent if children have run away because, for example, of domestic abuse.

### Confidentiality

The participants should be assured of confidentiality. This ensures the relationship of trust is not broken and a rapport can be built. As an example, when Willis was asked by the head whether he had seen who had written on the seats of a coach, he said he did not know. The reality was that he knew precisely who had done it, but his relationship with the 'lads' would have been badly affected had he 'informed' on them.

**Essential notes**

The BSA guidelines state: 'Guarantees of confidentiality and anonymity given to research participants must be honoured, unless there are clear and over-riding reasons to do otherwise'.

### Avoiding harm or danger of any sort

The researcher should ensure that participants will not be harmed by the research. They should also be careful not to put themselves in danger. Covert participant observation can be particularly problematic from the researcher's point of view. Patrick did not publish his research on the Glasgow street gang for six years for fear they might try to find him.

## Issues with confidentiality/avoiding harm

- Researchers have a dilemma when participants are harming themselves, e.g. taking drugs.
- There is a further issue when the participants intend to harm others.
- The extent to which research may harm the respondents may not initially be apparent. Israel and Hay found that a study of domestic violence in New Mexico was counter-productive in that the male abusers became even more abusive when they discovered their wives had taken part in the research.

### Key study

#### Colosi: A lap-dancer's ethical dilemmas

Colosi studied lap-dancers using ethnographic methods: participant observation and unstructured interviews. As a lap-dancer herself she had '**insider-status**' and was able to inform the other dancers and managers of the club that she was conducting research, but was unable to inform the ever-changing audience. A second ethical issue that arose was the use of cocaine by the dancers; this was both against the law and against club rules. However, in order to maintain her relationship with the other dancers, Colosi informed neither the police nor management.

**Source**: Colosi, R. *Doing ethnography: a lap-dancer's ethical dilemmas, Sociology Review*, 20:2 (2010)

In addition, most codes would include guidelines on the following:

- **Anonymity and privacy**
  This can be difficult when there are only a limited number of people in a particular role. For example, the staff from the school where Hargreaves carried out his research later said they knew when they read the research who some of the respondents were, because there were so few staff in the particular roles described.
- **The right to withdraw**
  Participants should be told of their right to withdraw at any stage.
- **The need to report illegal activities**
  Although most codes of ethics include this there is also a section on the professional integrity of the researcher.
- **Respondent validation**
  The participant's right to read what the researcher has written before publication can be problematic. Willis realized this when he asked the 'lads' to read his research and they said they understood what they had said but not what Willis had written about them.

The extent to which codes of ethics should be strictly followed is contested. Interpretive sociologists using covert methods argue their research would be affected by the Hawthorne effect if they followed the BSA guidelines in relation to informed consent.

Strict adherence would also mean that research of some deviant groups might never take place. Understanding of those groups would therefore be lost.

### Essential notes

Hobbs states that his research was unethical, but he engaged in illegal activities in order to remain 'involved'.

## Positivism and sociological research

Positivism has its roots in the work of the 19th century French sociologist, Comte. He argued that it was possible to study the social world using the methods of the natural sciences.

Positivists, in general, argue the following points:

- There are **social facts** that can be observed and studied. In addition, causal relationships can be sought. For example, unemployment is high in certain areas, and crime rates in these areas are also high. Is there a link?
- Social facts are external to individuals. Durkheim, another 19th century sociologist, decided to take the most personal of acts, suicide, and examine the extent to which it was an objective social fact.
- Society is more important than the individuals within society.
- Individuals are subject to external forces such as capitalism or competition in the education system.
- The social world is predictable.
- It is possible to study the social world in a logical and coherent way.
- It is possible to seek laws that govern people's behaviour.
- Research questions and hypotheses can be tested.

Popper and other social scientists who favour positivism now tend to opt for a hypothetico-deductive or deductive approach. They start with a theory and test it against evidence derived from research. This means that the researcher can generate a hypothesis or a research question based on observation or some previous evidence, and then conduct research to establish whether or not it is the case.

When conducting research, positivists want to do the following:

- Identify **patterns** and **trends**.
- Look for cause and effect.
- Identify what is predictable.
- Make comparisons over time and from one group to another and one culture to another. For example, the large-scale EU study on health, EPIC, which has been running for over 10 years in 10 European countries, involving 520 000 people, is in a position to make comparisons over time and across Europe.
- Look for **correlations**.
- Conduct research that can be tested and retested to check or confirm results in order to gain data that is **reliable**.
- Conduct research that is **objective** and **value-free**.
- Conduct large-scale data collection, so that it is safe to draw conclusions and make generalizations.
- Aim for consistency.

### The positivist research process

Positivists make a number of decisions before undertaking research.

- Choice of topic: this will depend on the funding source, and thus may not be a free choice.

- How to operationalize key ideas so that they can be measured: for example, research on poverty would need to start with a clear definition of what poverty is and where to draw the line.
- The hypothesis or research question: this is likely to be generated from observation of the social world and/or reading of previous research.
- Identifying a sampling technique in order to obtain a **representative** sample: this means that a **sampling frame**, if there is one, will need to be identified and access to it negotiated via a gatekeeper. For example, the head teacher of a school would be the gatekeeper if school registers were to be used as a sampling frame.
- Identifying a method that will obtain **quantitative data**.
- Deciding whether or not a **pilot study** should take place: most positivists, given the size of their research, are likely to do a pilot study.
- Identifying the location: for example, if structured interviews are to be used, where they will take place, or if questionnaires are to be used, how they will be distributed.
- How to record the data.
- How to analyse the data.

**Methods used by positivists**

Positivists seek quantitative data, so they use methods to produce and **replicate** this data, which include large-scale surveys, experiments, content analysis, comparative methods and official statistics.

**Characteristics of methods of collecting quantitative data**

- They produce numerical data.
- Graphs, tables and charts can be derived from the data, making comparisons and the identification of patterns and trends relatively straightforward.
- They tend to be high in reliability, though the measuring instrument should be standardized in order that the same or another researcher can conduct the research again to test it.
- They can be large scale and if the right sampling method is used, then it will be possible to gain a sample that is representative of the target population.
- It should be possible to make generalizations.

## Evaluation
- It has been argued that science itself is not objective and value-free.
- Humans have a free will and cannot be put in a laboratory.
- All variables in the social world cannot be controlled.
- Positivism ignores meanings and interpretations that people put on their actions, making it low in **validity**.
- It can identify where two facts are related but these facts may not be the cause and effect.
- Questionnaires are socially constructed, so are not objective or value-free.

**Examiners' notes**

While it is useful to know that positivists favour laboratory and field experiments, few sociologists use them and they are therefore not on your specification.

**Examiners' notes**

Students frequently confuse key concepts. To avoid this, think about the key concepts very carefully when you use them in an answer and never combine them in one sentence, as this usually demonstrates a lack of understanding.

### Essential notes

The structure versus **agency** debate is between those who argue that social structures shape our lives – not the exercise of free choice (agency).

## Interpretivism and sociological research

Interpretivism is sometimes referred to as anti-positivism. Weber, who was writing at the turn of the 19th and 20th centuries, was one of the main influences on its development.

Interpretivists argue the following points:

- Human beings are not inanimate. They have consciousness and therefore cannot be studied in the same way as phenomena in the natural world.
- It is not possible to identify cause and effect because human behaviour is unpredictable.
- The methods of the natural sciences are not appropriate when researching the social world because the social world is about meanings and human agency rather than social facts.
- People have subjective understandings of the structures of society. For example, young people have their own views and interpretations of the education system and act on the basis of these meanings. The meaning for a private school student on the way to Oxbridge will be quite different from the meaning for an underachieving student who is heading for the job market or unemployment.
- Findings are bound to be influenced by researchers' values; it is not possible to be **value-free**.
- The social world and the researcher affect each other.

Interpretivists also argue the social world does not exist outside of the social realities people construct. The researcher's task is to uncover the meanings and motives people attach to their actions and the actions of others. It is important to gain a rapport with the people being researched and then the data will increase in **validity**. Sociologists should try to 'walk' in the shoes of the people they are researching. This idea of *verstehen* comes from Weber and at a basic level means having an empathic understanding of people.

In carrying out research, interpretivists want to move from initial impressions to a deep understanding, recognizing that in so doing they are likely to find that their first impressions may be wrong in some way. Interpretivists also want to be reflective. Foster argues that this may help with the Hawthorne effect by reflecting on the extent behaviour will change as a result of the researcher's presence. **Reflexivity** is also about the researcher standing back and considering the research from her own perspective and as far as possible from the perspective of those being researched.

### Key study

Foster argues that her starting point in research is to understand the social world by observing and listening and 'seeking to understand the world from the point of view of the people in it'. She says that she likes to do qualitative research because it can help to explain people's behaviour and clarify the meaning of what might otherwise be misunderstood.

**Source:** Foster, J (2003), *Qualitative Research: Getting your pants dirty*, Sociology Review, Phillip Allan

## The interpretivist research process

In the research process, there is a need to identify the group or issue to research. There is also the need to work with a gatekeeper or use some other way to gain access to the group or individuals, and there is the need for a method to obtain qualitative data and where the research will take place.

In addition, researchers who collect qualitative data will need to think carefully about the ethics of the research.

### Research methods used by interpretivists

Methods used include **participant observation** and **unstructured interviews**, which are sometimes seen as being better than observation because the researcher can ask probing questions (if the subject matter is sensitive it might be the only way someone will talk), which will increase validity. Another method is **personal expressive documents**.

### Characteristics of methods used to collect qualitative data
- The data are in the form of words.
- They give an insight into the meanings people attach to their actions.
- They allow people to speak for themselves.
- They enable the researcher to do the research in the natural environment of the people they are researching, without disturbing their day-to-day behaviour too much.

## Evaluation
- Those being observed may be affected by the presence of the researcher, known as the **Hawthorne effect**.
- The social characteristics of a researcher may or will affect the research.
- It is important to know exactly how the researcher affects those with whom they are interacting.
- It is hard work, physically and emotionally; interpretivists often research vulnerable groups who are emotionally needy, such as Blackman's homeless in Brighton.
- Collecting **qualitative data** can be time-consuming.
- It is vital to keep good fieldwork notes.
- There is possibly the problem of **researcher imposition** and what data to select, which could affect validity.
- The research process and results may be subjective.
- The results will be low in **reliability**. There will no means of replicating the research.
- There is often a need for **respondent validation**, either with the individuals themselves or via other researchers.
- Researcher imposition may occur at the analysis stage.
- Qualitative research data cannot explain structural constraints.

### Essential notes

Foster points out that all researchers use their social characteristics. As a small middle-aged female, she had advantages which a tall young male may not have. However, he would have other advantages.

## Realism and sociological research

Realism is a view that arguably bridges the gap between positivism and interpretivism. Realists argue that:

- There are underlying **social structures**, and these can explain observable events.
- It should be possible to study the meanings people attach to actions, even if they are phenomena that cannot directly be observed. For example, it is not possible to observe **class consciousness**, but it is possible to observe its effects on whether people accept their position in society or not.

Realist sociologists believe that sociology can be scientific because of the difference between 'open' and 'closed' systems as objects of study. In closed systems all the variables can be controlled and measured, for example in some laboratory experiments in physics and chemistry. However, other sciences study open systems in which all the variables cannot be controlled, making predictions more difficult. For example, meteorologists are seen as scientists but they study an open system (the weather) so cannot make predictions with total certainty.

### Realism and sociology

Realists believe that sociology is scientific if it follows an 'open' system approach. Sociology must deal with what is observable, as well as with meanings that people attach to actions. There are social structures that lie beneath society's surface and these underpin the events that can be observed.

In carrying out research, realists want to:

- Understand the structural mechanisms that cannot be seen, such as **ideologies**, **false class consciousness** and the reproduction of the class system
- Be as objective, systematic and logical as possible within the constraint that the social world is not always based on logical and systematic principles
- Uncover underlying causal mechanisms that lead to observable events.

For example, sociologists might use realist techniques to explain how **capitalism** causes disruption in classrooms. Low-achieving students who misbehave on a regular basis may be doing so because of their awareness that there is no point in working because they will end up in jobs that do not require educational qualifications.

However, there may be deeper causes of their behaviour that are not directly observable. The capitalist system is based on a division of labour that requires a range of jobs, many of which are unskilled and low paid. Low-achieving pupils from working-class backgrounds are aware that they are destined for these positions. This way of thinking may lead to, or be a cause of, disruptive behaviour in the classroom.

## Essential notes

When Willis showed students his notes, the students said that they understood the parts where he quoted them verbatim but did not understand his explanations of the underlying mechanisms that made them act in the ways they did. School was not simply preparing them for labour, but was meeting capitalism's need for the workforce to be reproduced.

## Realist research

Realists believe that there is no such thing as theory-free data. They believe that theories and observable phenomena cannot be separated and that research should be based on the comparison and evaluation of theoretical ideas. They also believe that the purpose of research is to obtain data to test one theory against another theory. Some aspects of society are very difficult to quantify because they are happening at a deep level.

### The realist research process

The realist researcher decides on a problem, identifies the most likely theories to explain it and uses a range of methods to compare the theories with each other.

Realists often use a comparative approach. They also favour **mixed-methods** research which breaks down the division between **quantitative** and **qualitative** data.

Realists argue that research cannot be reliable because it is difficult to repeat. Churton argues that this is the same for much scientific research: '...in theory science insists on data being reliable...[but] ...it is rarely re-tested and is therefore no more reliable then the data collected from a one-off piece of sociological research.'

## Evaluation of realism

- Is realism just a new name for what a lot of sociologists have been doing for a while?
- There is no way of testing realist theories because they argue that sociological structures are like open systems in science: they cannot be observed.

### Essential notes

This is different to the positivist approach, which tests one theory using empirical data.

### Essential notes

Pawson argues that students should be cautious about setting **positivism** against **interpretivism** without considering possible alternatives, such as realism.

## Feminism and sociological research

Feminists believe that most sociological research reflects a **patriarchal** society and benefits men; it is what they call 'malestream'. Feminists have challenged 'malestream' research for a number of reasons:

- Research was focused on males and male activities. Studies often ignored or excluded women but generalized their findings to everyone.
- Aspects of social life such as domestic labour and childcare were ignored.
- Malestream sociological research methods focused on a so-called rational and scientific approach. This excluded female experiences.

### Feminist methodologies

There are various feminist methodologies.

- Interview techniques that break down the hierarchical nature of interviewer and interviewee and put an end to the power of the interviewer, leading to a more collaborative approach. This should increase validity but means that the researcher should be prepared to answer questions asked by the interviewee.
- **Reflexivity** is a concept used by Roberts, whereby researchers are more open and honest with their interviewees and also think about their own experiences when conducting the research.
- The use of methods that collect qualitative data. The argument is that quantitative data is inconsistent with feminist values and the objective of researching women's experiences.

However, there has been a shift of opinion by Oakley and others, and some feminists now suggest there should be a willingness to use the 'powerful' quantitative methods of data collection. Ramazanoghlu argues we need to be willing to use methods to suit the purpose. Skeggs agrees, arguing that quantitative data can be as useful as qualitative data.

### Evaluation

- Pawson argues that there is no new method; feminists use the usual range of methods and there are no particular innovations.
- Few researchers ultimately hand over power to the interviewees.
- Reflexivity is open to accusations of a lack of objectivity.
- Some researchers become over-involved with those being researched. Skeggs argues that this sometimes means the researcher must collude with comments she or he may not agree with.
- Oakley did break down the hierarchical relationship during her research with pregnant women. However, although she maintained contact with some of the women, she may have deceived others into thinking she had become a real friend and confidante.
- The relationship in an interview may be affected by class and ethnicity.

### The research topic

The feminist research topic should be:

- 'On, by and for women' (Stanley and Wise, 1983).
- Decided before any decisions are made about how to conduct the research.

- Relevant and sympathetic to women and women's experiences, as Skeggs tried to do and be, in her study with working-class women.
- Able to contribute to the exposure of women's oppression and help to end it; for example, gendered domestic roles.
- Able to help at an individual level. Some of Oakley's respondents said that taking part had 'reassured them of their normality'.
- Political, meaning it should raise awareness of issues pertinent to women, such as child sex abuse and domestic violence.
- Able to challenge male power and domination.

## Key study

Skeggs' study was based on 83 young working-class women. They had few educational qualifications but were all enrolled on care courses at a local further education college. Skeggs spoke to the women on numerous occasions over a 12-year period, exploring with them their experiences of being women as well as being working-class. She followed them into the labour market and when they began to have families. She found that they continually distanced themselves from their class origins and particularly from those who were not 'respectable'. Skeggs believes she did not exploit them and that they were able to feel good about themselves as a result of taking part in her study.

### Theoretical research issues
- Theory must come from the research and not determine it.
- Research should be more **interpretive** than **positivist**.
- It should always raise new questions rather than be viewed as an end in itself.

### Evaluation
- It could be argued that the researcher has a privileged ideologically-correct position, which may not be the view the interviewee wishes to take up.
- Cain and others argue that men must not be excluded, as Stanley and Wise imply (see page 78).
- Many of the strategies feminists use are also used by male sociologists such as Blackman, MacDonald and Craine, who have all done research with young people, including women.
- Feminist research is likely to have high **validity** but be low in **reliability**, because the nature of the relationship between the researcher and the researched will not be one that can be replicated.
- The people studied will be small in number and therefore may not be **representative**, making it difficult to **generalize**.

Despite criticisms, feminists have gone beyond what mainstream unstructured interviews would involve and radical feminists have researched and placed issues such as domestic violence firmly on the public agenda.

## Essential notes

Some researchers have had a similar experience to Skeggs, although Hobbs said he drew the line at racism, even knowing it could affect his status in the group.

**Source**: Skeggs, B (2001), *Women avoiding being working class* in Abercrombie, N and Warde, A, *The Contemporary Rustic Reader*

# General tips for the Exploring social inequality and difference exam (G674)

This unit is assessed through a two-hour examination paper with four questions to be answered. A total of 100 marks are available which means that, after reading time, there is a little more than one minute per mark. The paper consists of:

- Two compulsory methodological questions based on a supplied piece of source material drawn from practical research on social inequality and difference (this source material is not pre-released).

- A choice from two two-part questions on topics in social inequality and difference.

**Question 01** focuses on explaining the reasons for the use of a specific method or aspect of the research process in sociological research. Your answer should draw on both the source material and your wider knowledge. There are 10 marks available for knowledge and understanding (AO1) and 5 marks for interpretation and application (AO2a). Note that there are no evaluation (AO2b) marks for this question. You should try to refer to the source material as there may be advantages or reasons that you can select from this. AO2a marks are awarded for selection of relevant sociological evidence and for keeping your answer focused on the specific question. You should aim to spend approximately 20 minutes on this question.

For example, Question 01 may ask 'Outline and explain why pilot studies may be used in sociological research.' You need to focus on explaining why they are used and the advantages, and you must avoid writing about the disadvantages of the method or process.

**Question 02** is also a methods question, but the focus is upon the evaluation of an aspect of the research strategy, as outlined in the source material for a particular purpose. There are a total of 25 marks for this question, of which 5 marks are for AO1, 5 marks for AO2a and 15 marks are given for evaluation (AO2b). The question instruction will always be 'Outline and assess the view that ...' The emphasis is very much on evaluating and you are encouraged to use key methodological concepts to help you to weigh up the methods. For this question, you are expected to interpret and apply your knowledge and understanding to the method in the question. You must also ensure that you relate your knowledge to the context and aspect of social inequality under consideration, as given in the source material. You should spend approximately 30 minutes answering this question.

**Questions 03 (a)** and **04 (a)** require you to focus on describing the evidence for a broad aspect of social inequality and difference. There are 15 marks given for knowledge and understanding (AO1) and 5 marks for interpretation and application (AO2a). Note that there are no marks for analysis and evaluation, so you should avoid offering any criticism of the sociological evidence. This question will ask you to 'Outline the evidence for ...' and may refer to studies, statistical evidence and/or conceptual evidence. You should aim to spend approximately 25 minutes answering this question.

In this question, you are encouraged to refer to evidence of inequality from a range of areas of social life, including the workplace, education, health, welfare, family and politics. For example, if the question asked for evidence of female disadvantage, you may start with the family as an area of female disadvantage, but should include evidence about women and health, welfare, education and politics.

**Questions 03 (b)** and **04 (b)** ask you to evaluate sociological explanations of a broad aspect of social inequality and difference. This is a 40-mark essay question and will start with the instruction 'Outline and assess …' This question has 15 knowledge and understanding (AO1) marks, 5 interpretation and application (AO2a) marks and 20 analysis and evaluation (AO2b) marks. It is crucial, therefore, that you offer wide-ranging and detailed knowledge and evaluation of the theory in the question. You are expected to apply a wide range of theoretical interpretations to the view in the question, comparing and contrasting theories in an evaluative way. You should plan to spend 45 minutes answering this open-ended essay question.

# Exploring social inequality and difference (sample exam paper 1)

This piece of research is centred around the issue of young people's 'binge drinking' behaviour. Previous longitudinal research has shown that British young people aged 15 to 16 report the highest levels of drunkenness and positive attitudes to alcohol consumption in Europe. A normalized culture of intoxication is now central to many young people's social lives. This research examines the significance of alcohol consumption in the everyday lives of 'ordinary' young adult drinkers to explore the significance of loss of consciousness and loss of memory in their drinking stories. Through an analysis of focus group discussions with 89 young women and men aged 18 to 25, it explores the role of 'passing out stories' in relation to young people's alcohol consumption.

Drinking to excess remains heavily marked by gender, class and culture. Whilst young women's reported levels of frequent drinking and drunkenness are still less than those of their male peers, young women's rate and level of alcohol consumption has increased over the past two decades. However, drinking to excess is still associated with traditional and working-class forms of masculinity, whilst drunken women are still seen as sexually 'loose' and unfeminine.

This study explored the relationship between consumption and identity for young adults aged 18 to 25, focusing on accounts of 'everyday drinking' by 'ordinary' people, through 16 informal focus group discussions with 89 young adults. The focus groups were carried out in four different types of geographical locations, to make the sampling more representative. Participants were recruited through contacts with local colleges, and in most cases they were interviewed in friendship groups. Not all participants drank alcohol. Focus groups were facilitated by researchers in their twenties and thirties, with a view to putting participants at their ease when talking about their drinking practices, although the researchers were somewhat older than the respondents. Participants were informed that they were to be involved in a project looking at their social activities and were encouraged to talk about what they liked to do on a night out. Drinking was mentioned by participants as an important (although not essential) aspect of their social lives at an early stage in all the group discussions. Focus group sessions lasted between one and two hours and were recorded and subsequently transcribed.

The research participants recounted stories of drinking to the point of losing consciousness, losing their memory of events, vomiting, and waking up in hospital, representing their actions when drunk as beyond their control, awareness and responsibility. Some of these practices were constituted as excessive, undesirable, unpleasant or 'weird', but they were also recounted as a source of entertainment as part of a 'fun' night out in the context of a widespread culture of 'extreme drinking'.

**Source**: Griffin, C. et al. "Every Time I Do It I Absolutely Annihilate Myself": Loss of (Self) Consciousness and Loss of Memory in Young People's Drinking Narratives, *Sociology* 43: 457 (2009)

# Questions

Use the source material and your wider sociological knowledge to answer both questions 01 and 02.

**01** Outline and explain why some sociologists use representative sampling techniques. [**15 marks**]

**02** Outline and assess the view that focus groups are the best method of researching young people's views and stories about excessive alcohol consumption. [**25 marks**]

Using your wider sociological knowledge, answer question 03(a) and (b).

**03 (a)** Outline the evidence that females are disadvantaged in the contemporary UK. [**20 marks**]

**03 (b)** Outline and assess feminist explanations of gender inequality. [**40 marks**]

[**Total: 100 marks**]

## Grade A answer

**01** *Outline and explain why some sociologists use representative sampling techniques.* **[15 marks]**

This is a very good answer. The candidate clearly knows what a representative sampling technique is and links this to other research concepts, such as generalizability and validity. The response makes good use of the item, explaining how it was made more representative in geographical terms. This could, however, have been developed a little more; for example, what is it about doing research in just one geographical area that would make this particular research unrepresentative? How else did this researcher try to get a representative sample of young people? Wider knowledge and understanding is demonstrated at the end with the link to positivism.
**Marks: AO1 9/10, AO2a 4/5**
**Total = 13/15**

Using a representative sample means a researcher knows that the people whom they are studying are an accurate portrayal of their target population. To be representative a sample will have to contain characteristics of the people being studied, for example a similar proportion of different genders, ethnicities or geographical locations to the target population. This is shown in the binge drinking behaviour research, where they used four locations around the country to gain a representative sample. In doing this they established research which was not specific to one region of the country and could therefore be generalized from. It is important for sociological research to be representative because it means that their findings can be generalized to the target population. In other words, what is true of the sample population can be said to be true of the target population. If a study is not representative this also affects its validity as it is not giving a true picture of what it aimed to discover, as it will only represent the views of the limited sample being studied. This is sometimes referred to as population validity. The type of sociologists who prefer to use representative techniques are positivists because they like to be able to make large scale predictions and to develop cause and effect relationships. This cannot be done using a small unrepresentative sample.

**02** *Outline and assess the view that focus groups are the best method of researching young people's views and stories about excessive alcohol consumption.* **[25 marks]**

This is a very good paragraph. It's a good idea to define the method – this gains knowledge and understanding marks. There are consistent links to the context (both the research subjects and research topic) and accurate discussion of the key concept of validity, linked to insight.

Focus groups are a kind of group interview where the interviewer is a facilitator of the discussion which takes place between the members of the group. Focus groups can be a very useful method of gaining understanding of young people's attitudes and experiences of excessive alcohol consumption from a small group of participants at the same time. Focus groups allow for debate and discussion on the topic, which is useful as it is a topic which can be controversial and somewhat personal; through this method the interviewees are more likely to relax as they are in friendship groups so the researcher will be able to gain a fuller insight than may be gained from other methods. This means that the findings are more likely to be valid.

Another advantage of using a group of people together in research is that it allows the researcher access to a much larger sample in a short space of time than using a method such as individual interviews. This means more data can be gathered which, if the research is carried out appropriately, could lead to more representative data, as a larger sample will be able to offer a broader range of views on excessive alcohol consumption. Also, as focus groups gather rich qualitative data, they are more appropriate to research on views and stories about excessive alcohol consumption as it is easier to gather views, stories and opinions in depth through qualitative data than quantitative data; for example questionnaires would not have been able to offer the same level of information on what may be quite a complex topic. Once again, this adds to the validity of the research. Another reason why focus groups are most useful for researching young people's attitudes to alcohol is to reduce interviewer effect. As 'binge drinking' is a controversial subject, young people may not feel comfortable discussing it in a one-on-one interview, especially as the researcher is older than the interviewees. By using focus groups, young people are more likely to feel comfortable enough to be more open about their experiences with alcohol, therefore increasing the validity of the research.

However there are some weaknesses of this method. Firstly, the group environment of a focus group can reduce the validity of respondents' answers. They may feel under pressure to conform to the values of the rest of the group, therefore leading to research which is not giving a true picture of what they are trying to study. They may also be aware of the interviewer; for example the item states that the interviewer is an older person so they may feel uncomfortable discussing their experiences with them. This would be reduced by the other young people, however interviewer effect may still cause some reservations in their answers. Another issue with carrying out focus groups to research young people's experiences of excessive alcohol consumption is the lack of reliability. As people's experiences of drinking will be very unique, the data that is gathered will be different every time and therefore the reliability is significantly reduced. Positivists would criticize this lack of reliability as a research data collection technique that cannot be replicated is not very useful. There is also the issue of the sample. It is still a relatively small sample which means that the results gathered may not be representative of the target population of young people and therefore may not be able to be generalized from.

An explicit evaluation of the method in the question. There is a range of evaluation points made with links to theory and to concepts. There are explicit links made with the context. Overall, there is a wide range of knowledge, understanding and evaluation. It would have been useful to offer a conclusion; this would have pushed it into the top band. **Marks: AO1 4/5, AO2a 4/5, AO2b 12/15 Total = 20/25**

This response shows an excellent knowledge and understanding of how females are disadvantaged. The knowledge is appropriate and wide ranging (there are references to five areas of social life). It is also accurate and detailed (each area of social life is well explained) and is both conceptual and empirical. The response demonstrates a depth of sociological understanding and a holistic approach, in terms of linking different areas of the specification. This response shows an excellent ability to interpret sociological knowledge and understanding and apply it to the area of female disadvantage.

**Marks: AO1 15/15, AO2a 5/5 Total = 20/20**

**03 (a)** *Outline the evidence that females are disadvantaged in the contemporary UK.* **[20 marks]**

Whilst women have many more rights than they have had in the past, there are a number of areas of society where they experience disadvantage. One of these is the roles they are now expected to undertake both in the workplace and the home. According to Dunscombe and Marsden, women are expected to take on a 'triple shift' which involves three roles of housework, paid work and emotion work. This means that they are not only expected to perform to the same standard as men in the workplace, but also to keep up with the housework and childcare. Research carried out by Seager through the use of time diaries found that whilst men spent more time at work, they still had more leisure and rest time than women.

Within the workplace it has been proven that over a lifetime the cost of being female in Britain is nearly 50% less income than a male. Feminists note that the workplace is patriarchal in two main ways: vertical and horizontal segregation. Vertical segregation refers to the 'glass ceiling', whereby men advance over women within industries. Despite the fact women make up 45% of the workforce there is a low concentration of them at the top levels; for example they only make up 9% of top company directors and 6% of high court judges. This lack of women advancing is a clear example of female disadvantage. Horizontal segregation refers to men and women being located in different types of occupations. Statistics show that women are more likely to be confined to less well paying industries, such as nurses and hairdressers. In 2008 just 126 out of 646 MPs were women, offering another example of how men dominate the better paid occupations.

The rise of divorce has, arguably, led to disadvantage for women in the UK. Over 90 per cent of lone-parent families are headed by females and these are much more likely to experience poverty than other family types. This shows the disadvantage that women suffer as they are left with no money to bring up children in poor conditions. This poverty is made worse by the fact that women tend to get paid less than men and are more likely to be found in temporary, part time work. In fact, according to Peter Townsend, such is the extent that women find themselves in most groups which experience poverty that he labels it the 'feminization of poverty'.

Women also suffer disadvantage in the area of health. It is well documented that women suffer higher levels of illness than men. In particular, they are more likely to suffer from mental illnesses, especially anxiety and depression. This may be linked with some of the factors already discussed such as the stress brought on by undertaking the triple shift or the experience of suffering poverty. Women are more likely to suffer eating disorders as, according to feminists such as Orbach, they feel pressurized by a media which supports the ideal 'size zero' figure.

Women can also be said to be disadvantaged in terms of crime. Feminists argue that women are likely to be treated more harshly by the criminal justice system compared to men. According to Heidensohn, the courts treat females more harshly than males particularly when they deviate from gender norms. ☞

For example, there is a double standard operating in the courts which punish girls but not boys for promiscuous sexual activity. Pat Carlen puts forward a similar view in relation to prison sentences. She argues that when women are jailed, it is less for the 'seriousness of their crimes and more according to the court's assessment of them as wives, mothers and daughters'.

**03 (b)** *Outline and assess feminist explanations of gender inequality.*
**[40 marks]**

Feminists work to try and gain equality between men and women and to ensure women receive the same rights as men. Feminist sociologists mainly research the effect of gender on an individual's role, status and life chances in society. Most believe women are disadvantaged in society due to their gender and that this disadvantage is socially constructed. There are a number of different types of feminist which all have very different approaches to the topic, including liberal feminism, Marxist feminism, radical feminism and postmodern feminism.

Liberal feminists work to ensure equal opportunities between men and women. They believe that rather than being judged on gender, people should be judged meritocratically. Women should compete with men freely without gender playing a part. Whilst they have been very successful in campaigning for acts involving equal pay and sexual discrimination, they still believe there is a high level of inequality, particularly in the workplace, which needs to be challenged by changing views and implementing more anti-discrimination legislation. In one sense, liberal feminism can be seen as an attack on functionalism. Parsons, a functionalist, argued that men should take on the instrumental, breadwinner role and women are better suited to taking on expressive roles; ones which involve emotion, attachment and subjectivity. Liberal feminists, however, challenge this division and argue that women and men are equally capable of performing roles in both spheres and that traditional gender separated roles stop both men and women from leading fulfilling lives.

The main strength of liberal feminism is that it has helped to highlight the idea that gender differences are not inborn but are the result of different treatment and socialization patterns. However, liberal feminists are criticized for being over-optimistic. They ignore the possibility that there are deep-seated structures causing women's oppression such as capitalism or patriarchy. Marxist feminists and radical feminists argue that liberal feminism fails to recognize the underlying causes of women's subordination and that it is too simplistic to believe that changes in the law or social attitudes will be enough to bring equality. Instead, they believe that drastic revolutionary change is needed.

Radical feminists believe society is dominated by patriarchy and male control. They believe all women are oppressed and exploited by men and therefore advocate separatism whereby women separate themselves completely from men, sexually and socially. Men are seen to seize all material gains and social privileges and deny these to women. Radical feminists do not believe ☞

This is a very good, analytical introduction which explains the main feminist standpoint and introduces the common strands of feminism. It is conceptual, and it also sets out to 'signpost' the essay; that is, the reader can tell where this essay is going through reading this introductory paragraph.

This is a good explanation of liberal feminism with some concepts used accurately. It would, however, benefit from more depth; for example, by explaining how liberal feminists see gender roles as socially constructed and transmitted through socialization. There is an analytical tone when comparing functionalism and liberal feminism.

This is an excellent evaluative and analytical paragraph. It pulls out the main strengths of the theory before explaining the key weakness. This is a sophisticated response which links the criticisms to other feminist perspectives.

This is another good paragraph, focusing on radical feminism. The theory is well explained and conceptually strong, although it could have offered further depth and detail by including some more studies and, for example, looking at radical feminists' proposals for change. The criticisms are explicit, but underdeveloped and a little vague.

This paragraph focuses on another feminist explanation. It is a well explained paragraph, using concepts such as the reserve army of labour. It could have been further developed by, for example, including an explanation of the ideological role of familialism. The criticisms are explicit, but again, underdeveloped. Instead of writing 'other feminists', the candidate should include specific alternative theories and/or studies.

This is a good final paragraph, leading to a conclusion which offers a range of points of criticism from other perspectives, although it is a little list-like and underdeveloped. It is a good idea to bring the debate into the contemporary realm by using phrases such as 'more recently'. There is an attempt at an explicit conclusion although it is a little vague.

the differences in nature between men and women which are presented as biological are so and instead believe them to be social constructs. For radical feminists, patriarchal oppression is direct and personal. It occurs not only in public, but also in the private area of the family and relationships. Radical feminists, such as Brownmiller, argue that domestic violence and rape is a visible form of patriarchy. Even the threat of it is a powerful way of controlling women. However radical feminism has been highly criticized, as many sociologists believe it to be too extreme a view and think there are other factors which affect gender inequality. They argue that women's position in society has improved vastly since the beginning of the feminist movement and that segregation between men and women would not improve society.

Another type of feminism is Marxist feminism, which combines Marx's theory of the economy with feminism. They believe that women's roles as housewives helped sustain a culture of capitalism and focus on women's economic role in society. One issue they raised was women being reliant on their husband's wages and being unpaid for housework and childcare. As capitalism is a competitive system where people are being put against each other constantly, they believe women are used to compete against men unfairly. Marx's theory of the reserve army of labour explains this, when he says there is a reserve of people whose jobs are unstable and less well paid who are only important for economic booms. Marxist feminists, such as Beechey, believe the reserve army of labour is mainly occupied by women, who are seen to be mainly reliant on their husband's wages and therefore not an important part of the labour market. However the Marxist feminist theory can be criticized as being outdated, as much of it seems to ignore the vast improvement in women's place in the workforce. Other feminists have also criticized it for focusing too heavily on the economic role and thereby ignoring other important areas of discrimination.

However other sociologists do not agree with the feminist view. Functionalists believe that men and women's roles in society are natural and functional and that for society to work as it does, men and women's roles should remain how they are. They state that it is biology for men and women to behave in a different manner and therefore occupy different roles in society. Marxists and Weberians also believe that feminists do not pay enough attention to the role of the economy. More recently, there has been an attack on these traditional feminist theories which all assume that all women share a similar situation and similar experience of oppression. By contrast, 'difference feminists' do not see women as a single homogenous group. They argue that middle-class and working-class women, white and black women, lesbian and heterosexual women have very different experiences and can not all be lumped together as one group. Therefore whilst feminism can offer some explanation into understanding gender inequality it lacks in other areas and so cannot offer us a full understanding.

Overall, this response demonstrates knowledge which is appropriate, wide ranging, accurate and detailed, with some reference to theoretical/empirical studies. However, it lacks depth and is a little vague in parts; for example, more reference is needed to specific studies which means it is not a top level response. In terms of analysis and evaluation, this is probably the weakest skill area. This response demonstrates good ability to evaluate and analyse feminist explanations by raising some precise points, but many of these are left undeveloped and unexplored. There is some comparison and contrasting of different theoretical positions, but it is not developed or wide ranging. The evaluation is not sustained.
**Marks: AO1 12/15, AO2a 4/5, AO2b 12/20 Total = 28/40**

**Overall marks – 81/100 = Grade A**

# Exploring social inequality and difference (sample exam paper 2)

This study, by Ball and Vincent, draws on data collected from an ESRC funded qualitative project to highlight the enthusiasm of middle-class parents for enrolling their under-fives in 'enrichment' activities (extra-curricular creative and sporting classes). Ball and Vincent seek to identify the part activities play in parental strategies for class reproduction. Their study considers the broader issue of children and consumption, drawing out the way in which consumption and leisure activities are highly classed, and focusing on ideas of taste and distinction. Secondly, using examples from the data, they emphasize the sense of urgency and responsibility parents felt concerning their child's development and the classed and gendered involvement of parents.

The study uses material from interviews with 57 mothers and 14 fathers (from 59 different middle-class families) in two localities in middle-class areas of London. The researchers employed a variety of methods to find a sample of respondents, including placing adverts in child-friendly shops and cafés, and in local area parenting and National Childbirth Trust (NCT) newsletters. They also attended preschool activity sessions (e.g. music, library story-time), and 'snowballed' from their initial contacts. All families had at least one preschool child, ranging in ages from a few months to five years. They conducted repeat interviews with 20 mothers, nine of which included their partners. The respondent parents were a singular group, being largely white (except three), in heterosexual relationships (except one), and highly educated (52 mothers and 52 fathers had at least a first degree).

As part of their in-depth interviews, Ball and Vincent asked how the children spent their days, what they did, either at home with the mother or carer, or in another care setting. Parents whose children attended nursery often mentioned the 'extras', now routinely included by private day care providers (but often at extra cost), such as French, music, or (more unusually) yoga. They also specifically asked respondents whether their children were involved in any other such activities outside nursery. In nearly every case they were, and activities ranged from ballet and gymnastics to singing, French and piano; all at a relatively high cost.

Ball and Vincent conclude that enrichment activities are one response to the anxiety and sense of responsibility experienced by middle-class parents as they attempt to 'make up' a middle-class child in a social context where reproduction appears uncertain.

Source: Ball, S. and Vincent, C. "Making up" the middle-class child: Families, activities and class dispositions' *Sociology* 41: 1061 (2007).

# Questions

Use the source material and your wider sociological knowledge to answer both questions 01 and 02.

**01** Outline and explain why some sociologists use a 'variety of methods to find a sample'. [**15 marks**]

**02** Outline and assess the view that in-depth interviews are the best method of researching middle-class parents' reasons for providing enrichment activities for their young children. [**25 marks**]

Using your wider sociological knowledge answer questions 03(a) and (b).

**03 (a)** Outline the evidence of middle-class advantage in the contemporary UK. [**20 marks**]

**03 (b)** Outline and assess functionalist explanations of social inequality. [**40 marks**]

[**Total: 100 marks**]

**Grade C answer**

**01** *Outline and explain why some sociologists use a 'variety of methods to find a sample'.* [15 marks]

This is an accurate explanation of why some sociologists use a variety of sampling techniques with some good use of key concepts (sampling frame, representativeness). There is reference to the source study, but there are some opportunities missed. For example, the absence of a sample frame could have been discussed in the context of this specific study and the reasons for using a snowball sampling method could have been related to the characteristics of participants in this study. It also lacks in terms of range of knowledge and understanding – there are only two reasons explained; the answer offers some depth but not range.
**Marks: AO1 6/10, AO2a 3/5**
**Total = 9/15**

Sampling is the process of selecting a group of respondents to study from a target population. There are many ways to do this. One reason why some sociologists may use a variety of methods is that the researcher doesn't have a sampling frame or list of suitable respondents to choose from, making accessing a sample more difficult. A sampling frame, such as a school register, is used for random and stratified random sampling. The researcher may not have access to this list as they may need a gatekeeper, a person who has access to the desired participants. In order to obtain a sample without a sampling frame, other methods of sampling must be used.

Another reason for using more than one method of sampling is that some methods have weaknesses, so a different technique is used to cancel out the problems. For example, Ball and Vincent used snowball sampling, but this creates a very unrepresentative sample, drawing on participants from interlinked social circles with not everyone having a fair chance to contribute to the research. To increase the representativeness of the study, Ball and Vincent also used volunteer sampling by using adverts in the local area and in newsletters in two different locations. This meant that they could access a wider audience; however, this may only appeal to a certain type of person.

**02** *Outline and assess the view that in-depth interviews are the best method of researching middle-class parents' reasons for providing enrichment activities for their young children.* [25 marks]

This paragraph demonstrates a very good knowledge and understanding of unstructured interviews and the main strengths. There is accurate discussion of key concepts, theory and links to other research. However, there is a lot of missed opportunity for contextualizing the response. The candidate needed to relate these strengths to this particular research context; for example, what is it about interviewing middle-class parents that might make this method useful? ☞

In-depth interviews are a useful method of researching middle-class parents' reasons for providing their children with enrichment activities as they tend to be less structured and intimidating to the respondent as the researcher holds less control over the flow of the conversation and topic. As this research requires rich, detailed qualitative data about parents' motives behind providing their children with free time activities, in-depth, unstructured interviews are an ideal method as they allow free expression of thoughts, feelings and opinions, increasing the validity of the findings. In unstructured interviews, a rapport is established which further increases the validity. This method is useful as areas of ambiguity can be clarified due to the relaxed, natural nature of these interviews in comparison to more structured methods; however, the majority of control lies with the respondent. This means the researcher is less likely to impose their own values on the research, creating a more truthful picture in its findings. It may also mean that there is a more equal balance of power between the sociologist and the respondent. Finally, there is a possibility that participants ☞

may produce information that the researcher was not expecting and may reflect ideas that the researchers would not have thought to ask about. This advocates an Interpretivist approach, favoured by sociologists such as Charlesworth, Skeggs and Thiel who use similar methods to also study class and experience.

The research states that Ball and Vincent are seeking qualitative data through these interviews; however, Positivists would point out that this method will lack reliability due to possible interviewer effects and the inconsistent nature of interviews. For these reasons, validity may also be reduced as a result of desirability or wanting to impress the researcher and give the answers they think the sociologists would want. As the study is about parenting and family, the respondents would want to appear to be good parents and so may alter their answers. As it looks at family, there is a small possibility that an issue raised may touch a nerve with a participant. This could further affect validity but also raises ethical issues around the protection of participants from psychological harm. A better method for researching middle-class parents' reasons for providing children with enrichment activities may be questionnaires as participants may disclose more if they know their responses are anonymous. This method, favoured by Positivists who look for social patterns rather than deep feeling, would be less time consuming and would allow the researcher to study a larger sample more efficiently. It would also increase reliability, as this is an easy method to repeat and still obtain the same results, whilst reducing possible interviewer effects.

It may be useful to use methodological pluralism and combine methods so that the weaknesses of one method can be combined with the strengths of another.

What is it about studying enrichment activities that may make this method a strong one?

This is a very good paragraph outlining the main weaknesses. It is theoretical and conceptual and is much better at engaging with the context than the first half of this answer.

Overall, this answer demonstrates a good level of knowledge and understanding of the method and its strengths and weaknesses. It shows a very good ability to evaluate and analyse the view in the question. There is an attempt to draw a conclusion but it is underdeveloped. The evaluation is sustained, though lacking depth and/ or detail at times. The discussion is explicitly related to the research context but it is not balanced throughout.
**Marks: AO1 4/5, AO2a 3/5, AO2b 10/15 Total = 17/25**

---

**03 (a)** *Outline the evidence of middle-class advantage in the contemporary UK.* [**20 marks**]

There is evidence to suggest that the middle class are more advantaged in comparison to other classes in the contemporary UK.

In terms of education, the middle class are advantaged and have higher life chances. Children born into lower-class families only have a 1% chance of going to university while those with professional parents have a 73% chance of going. There is also evidence of a direct correlation between social class and educational qualifications gained and school leaving age, so those further down the class scale are more likely to leave school at a younger age with fewer formal qualifications. This is a reflection of their cultural and economic ☞

capital as sociologists have found that middle-class parents spend more time involved in their children's education and have more confidence when interacting with teachers in comparison to working-class parents.

Health also shows that the middle classes are advantaged. The Acheson Report found that only 17% of professional men and 25% of professional women reported long-standing illnesses. This was higher for unskilled workers – 48% for men and 45% for women. Over recent years, life expectancy has increased for all but especially for the middle classes. Between 1972–76 and 1992–96, the life expectancy gap between professionals and unskilled, manual men grew from 5.5 years to 9.5 years. This was also the case for women. There is also an apparent geographical class divide with a 10.5 year life expectancy gap between men from Blackpool and those from Chelsea and Kensington. Death rates also reflect middle-class advantage. Evidence shows that unskilled, manual workers are twice as likely to die before professional men. Infant mortality is also twice as frequent in the working class compared to the middle class. Unskilled workers are four times more likely to commit suicide than professionals. This shows a link between income, wealth, life chances and general happiness.

> This demonstrates good sociological knowledge and understanding of middle-class advantage. There is statistical, conceptual and empirical evidence offered in support of this. However, it lacks in range. There are really only two areas of social life used: health and education. This is, therefore, a Level 3 response which demonstrates depth but not range.
> **Marks: AO1 8/15, AO2a 4/5**
> **Total = 12/20**

---

**03 (b)** *Outline and assess functionalist explanations of social inequality.*
**[40 marks]**

Social inequality refers to any difference between groups or individuals in society which results in one having inferior life chances than the other. Functionalists believe these inequalities are the result of the meritocracy we live in. This is a system based on the idea that social stratification is necessary and desirable for society.

> It is a good idea to define key words in the essay question. However, the candidate could have explained the background to functionalist theory in general.

Functionalists believe social stratification is both inevitable and beneficial to everyone in society. This perspective sees a meritocracy as desirable because it filters out the most talented from the least talented. All negative aspects of the meritocratic system are ignored, with only the positive outcomes being focused on. Functionalists argue that a meritocratic system works and continues because of the value consensus which means that people do not challenge the system.

> An attempt at explaining how stratification is desirable but it is very underdeveloped and vague – particularly in relation to the value consensus idea.

Davis and Moore are functionalists who have studied the meritocracy we live in. They believe role allocation is vital as society places the most suitable people in the most important jobs. Higher rewards are used for these important jobs to attract the best people and to motivate others to try and move up and down the meritocratic system. Davis and Moore argued that people would be unlikely to work really hard and defer gratification if there weren't unequal rewards attached at the end of it. For example, doctors have to go to university for at least seven years. They will not want to do this unless they have the reward of high status and pay at the end of it. This inevitably causes inequality. ☞

> This is a reasonable explanation of Davis and Moore's theory. It is, however, lacking in depth. For example, it doesn't explain why some jobs are functionally more important.

The ideas of the New Right are similar to Functionalism. They also believe that the people at the top of the social stratification system have a higher output and deserve the higher rewards. This contrasts to what New Right thinkers such as Murray describe as the underclass, who hold little merit and so deserve their position lower down the system and the fewer rewards to match that position. Murray believes this separate underclass to be work shy, promiscuous, criminal, and welfare dependent.

However, Functionalism can be criticized in many ways. Firstly, Functionalists assume a general value consensus that all abide by, but Marxists argue that it isn't a value consensus, but ruling class ideology which keeps people in their place. They also ignore other motives people might have to work such as pride or a sense of service and assume that everyone works for material or monetary rewards. Most importantly, Functionalists ignore all the negative effects of a meritocracy.

Marxists are also structuralists. Marxists believe capitalism is creating social inequality as the classes are polarizing or growing further apart due to the conflict between them. The capitalist system creates class conflict by allowing the bourgeoisie to exploit and oppress the proletariat, creating a hierarchy. In contrast to Functionalists that believe the system remains due to a value consensus, Marxists believe this is due to a false class consciousness that leads people to believe the system is fair. However, Marxism can be criticized as its initial ideas as set out by Karl Marx have not been fulfilled as there has not been a proletarian revolution.

Weberian theory is a social action theory. It doesn't simply focus on the relationship to someone's means of production but it looks at the distinction between class, status and party as three separate but related sources of power which affect life chances. Class, your position in the economic market place, will vary according to income and skill as Weber believes that there are many small occupational classes in society. Status refers to the competition between classes for greater honour. This is a clear indicator of inequality as one social group will certainly have less than another. This is also the case with party, which refers to access to power. Weber, however, is criticized as being too complex in identifying numerous classes.

In conclusion, we have to ask whether class is still a signficant division in society. Postmodernists would argue that class is dead as a result of increasing freedom and diversity. Feminists would argue that gender inequality is a more significant division than class inequality.

It is a good idea to introduce New Right theories here, but again it needs to be explained in more depth. For example, how do functionalist and New Right theories differ?

This paragraph is an explicit evaluation of the functionalist view, but the points are underdeveloped. For example, how is value consensus linked to explanations of inequality? What are the negative effects of meritocracy?

This is evaluation by using an alternative theory. There is some good contrast of theories which displays analysis skills but there is also some juxtaposition. Alternative theories need to be directly contrasted with functionalism.

This paragraph is explicit evaluation of the functionalist view but the points are underdeveloped. For example, how is value consensus linked to explanations of inequality? What are the negative effects of meritocracy?

Again, this is evaluation in the sense of offering an alternative theory; but it is juxtaposition as it is not linked to functionalism.

It is good to see an attempt at an explicit conclusion but it needs to be developed further in relation to the main strengths and weaknesses of functionalism.

Overall, this is a Level 3 response. There is some knowledge and understanding of functionalism which is more than basic. There are accurate uses of concepts, theories and studies but they are mainly underdeveloped and lacking depth. There are some explicit points of evaluation, but again they are undeveloped and with a lot of juxtaposition.

**Marks: AO1 9/15, AO2a 3/5, AO2b 10/20 Total = 22/40**

**Overall marks – 60/100 = Grade C**

# Improving your grade

The following examples show how you can improve your answers to the first question for the Exploring social inequality and difference paper. The question is from paper 2 (see page 90).

01 *Outline and explain why some sociologists use a 'variety of methods to find a sample'.* **[15 marks]**

## Weak answer

Sampling methods are used to select a sub-section of the group being studied. Sociologists use a variety of methods to find a sample because often they want a big sample so if they use different methods they can get a larger sample. Larger samples are good as they are representative and can be generalized. For example, if you want to get a sample of children, you could get some from a school, some from a youth club and some from hanging around places that young people visit. Some sociologists also use a variety of methods such as interviews or questionnaires, this also means that the researcher can build up a bigger sample. Another reason for using different samples is because the researchers might not agree on which is the best sampling method as some sampling methods are seen as better than others.

This is a basic response which is largely based on practical issues, such as getting a large sample or accessing different groups of people. There is some reference to concepts (representativeness, generalizability) but they are undeveloped and not explained. The real weakness is the lack of reference to the source. An example is given about accessing children, but this research was about middle-class parents. It is also somewhat simplistic; it is unlikely that different sampling methods will be chosen because of a lack of agreement amongst researchers! It is also confused and starts talking about research methods, rather than sampling methods.
**Marks: AO1 4/10, AO2a 2/5
Total = 6/15**

## Better answer

Sampling is the process of selecting a group of respondents to study from a target population. There are many ways to do this. One reason why some sociologists may use a variety of methods is that the researcher doesn't have a sampling frame or list of suitable respondents to choose from, making accessing a sample more difficult. A sampling frame, such as a school register, is used for random and stratified random sampling. The researcher may not have access to this list as they may need a gatekeeper, a person who has access to the desired participants. In order to obtain a sample without a sampling frame, other methods of sampling must be used. ☞

This is an accurate explanation of why some sociologists use a variety of sampling techniques with some good use of key concepts (sampling frame, representativeness). There is reference to the study in the Item, but there are some opportunities missed. For example, the absence of a sampling frame could ☞

have been discussed in the context of this specific study and the reasons for using a snowball sampling method could have been related to the characteristics of participants in this study. It also lacks in terms of range of knowledge and understanding – there are only two reasons explained; the answer offers some depth but not range.
**Marks: AO1 6/10, AO2a 3/5
Total = 9/15**

Another reason for using more than one method of sampling is that some methods have weaknesses, so a different technique is used to cancel out the problems. For example, Ball and Vincent used snowball sampling, but this creates a very unrepresentative sample, drawing on participants from interlinked social circles with not everyone having a fair chance to contribute to the research. To increase the representativeness of the study, Ball and Vincent also used volunteer sampling by using adverts in the local area and in newsletters in two different locations. This meant that they could access a wider audience.

### Good answer

Sampling is the process of selecting a group of respondents to study from a target population. There are many ways to do this and sociologists usually distinguish between representative and non-representative sampling techniques. One reason why some sociologists may use a variety of methods is that the researcher doesn't have a sampling frame or list of suitable respondents to choose from, making accessing a sample more difficult. A sampling frame is used for random and stratified random sampling but the researcher may not have access to this list so they may need a gatekeeper, a person who has access to the desired participants, or the list may not exist. For example, this piece of research is about middle-class parents and there is no readily available sample frame. In order to obtain a sample without a sampling frame, other methods of sampling must be used, as shown in Ball and Vincent's study which used local adverts and newsletters to attract a sample.

This is a very good answer, showing range and depth of knowledge and understanding; there are a number of clear reasons which are all well explained. Therefore, this answer displays both depth and range. In terms of interpretation and application, this answer is well focused on the source material and makes constant reference to the group being studied – middle-class parents. The answer contains well explained references to key concepts, particularly representativeness.
**Marks: AO1 10/10, AO2a 5/5
Total = 15/15**

Another reason for using more than one method of sampling is that some methods have more weaknesses, so a different technique is used to cancel out the problems. For example, Ball and Vincent used snowball sampling. This method is ideal for this case as the study is very specifically focused on middle-class parents of young children and one respondent is likely to be able to put the researcher in touch with a similar participant through their own personal contacts and social networks; however, this creates a very unrepresentative sample, drawing on participants from interlinked social circles with not everyone having a fair chance to contribute to the research. To increase the representativeness of the study, Ball and Vincent also used volunteer sampling by using adverts in the local area and in newsletters in two different locations. This meant that they could access a wider audience; however, this may only appeal to a certain type of person so, again, it could prove to be lacking in representativeness.

Another reason why Ball and Vincent may have used these different sampling techniques is just to access a larger sample; if they just relied on snowball sampling, they might not have got many referrals so they backed it up with the volunteer adverts. They also wanted to target different geographical middle-class areas, to try and improve representativeness, so again, this would have been difficult by just relying on a snowball sample.

Overall, some sociologists will use a variety of methods to find a sample in order to make it more representative and, therefore, generalizable, access a larger sample or overcome problems when sampling such as limited access, no sampling frame or gatekeeper or flawed methodology.

| | |
|---|---|
| **Access** | Being able to get in touch with the group or population that is to be studied – sometimes difficult when the group is closed or 'deviant' |
| **Age discrimination** | Unfavourable treatment of an age group because of their age – usually applies to the elderly |
| **Agency** | The ability to make choices about social actions, e.g. to construct and reconstruct social identities |
| **Age patriarchy** | The way in which older people exercise power over the young in a variety of ways, including legislation |
| **Alienation** | The way in which workers experience their work as separate from themselves; work does not satisfy them or their inherent creativity |
| **Assimilation** | The theory that minority ethnic groups would take on the culture of the dominant group and be assimilated |
| **Attrition** | Usually linked to longitudinal studies, it is the loss of sampling units from the sample group as a result of moving away, death or loss of interest |
| **Boundary problem** | The question of who should and who should not be included in the middle class, where to draw the line |
| **Bourgeoisie** | A Marxist term for the owners of the means of production, the capitalist class |
| **Canalization** | The process of channelling children's interests to gender-specific toys |
| **Capitalism** | An economic system in which goods and services are produced for profit |
| **Case study** | The detailed study of a social group, an individual, an event or an institution |
| **Causal links** | The way(s) in which one thing may be associated with another, e.g. rising unemployment with boys' underachievement at school |
| **Causal relationship** | The way one variable may result from another, e.g. boys' educational under-achievement may be partly the result of rising unemployment |
| **Class consciousness** | A Marxist concept, it is the ways in which a social class is aware of their shared common interests, e.g. the working class and the exploitation they experience or the upper class who have a shared interest in remaining an elite group |
| **Cohort study** | Research on people who share a certain characteristic – often age; the National Child Development Study was based on all the children born in one week in March 1958 |
| **Collective conscience** | A concept used by Durkheim to mean the common beliefs and values of a society |
| **Comparisons** | To compare data or material from different studies |
| **Concrete ceiling** | Relates to the experiences of black and Asian women who are not told about opportunities they might aspire to, and so cannot see through a 'glass ceiling' |
| **Conflict view** | A theory stating that society is made up of groups who have fundamentally different interests |
| **Consensus** | The view that most people in society share the same norms and values |
| **Contradictory class position** | Associated with Wright, a neo-Marxist who argues that managers find themselves caught between the bourgeoisie who exploit them and the proletariat whom they control |

| Correlation | The tendency for one thing to be found with another, e.g. children who are in poverty do less well in education |
|---|---|
| Covert observations | Observation where the researcher does not reveal that they are a researcher |
| Crisis of masculinity | Used to describe the confusion and uncertainty that some men, particularly young men, allegedly feel about their place in society, what their role is as the labour market shifts from heavy manufacturing to the service sector |
| Cultural capital | Advantages derived from the possession of middle-class knowledge, language, experiences, attitudes and values |
| Cultural constraints | The ways in which some groups, who do not possess the dominant cultural capital, are less likely to do as well, e.g. in the education system, which is based on the culture of the middle classes |
| De-skilling | The removal of skill from work as a result of technology |
| Disconnected | The ways in which some groups are marginalized by society and experience, often unwillingly; a separation from mainstream society |
| Discrimination | The unfavourable treatment of one group compared to another |
| Dominant culture | The norms, values, experiences and language skills of the ruling class |
| Dominant ideology | The ideas of the ruling class, which pervade society |
| Dominant patriarchal ideology | The ideas of the male-dominated society are those that over-ride all others |
| Dual labour market | The theory that there are two labour markets – the primary labour market where jobs are secure and the secondary labour market in which jobs are less secure and often part-time or casual |
| Economic capital | The possession of wealth and income |
| Edgework | Lyng's term for risky behaviour of young males, e.g. speeding |
| Educational achievement | The educational levels and/or qualifications achieved by individuals or groups |
| Educational underachievement | Individuals or groups who do not reach their potential in the educational system |
| Elite | Those who are viewed as the highest and most talented in society; also refers to the most powerful |
| Elite self-recruitment | The way(s) in which those at the top of society work to ensure that new recruits come from within their own class |
| Embourgeoisement | A process of taking on the characteristics of the bourgeoisie, or middle class, in terms of culture, values and beliefs; the embourgeoisement theory was tested by Goldthorpe and Lockwood on the car workers in Luton in the 1960s |
| Equal opportunities | The treatment of everyone in society in a fair and just way, irrespective of their class, gender, ethnicity, age and other social characteristics |
| Ethics | The moral rights and wrongs in relation to the conduct of research, e.g. those being studied should be assured of confidentiality, anonymity and the right to withdraw at any stage |
| Ethnicity | A person's cultural background, often associated with race and/or nationality |

| | |
|---|---|
| **Ethnic penalty** | The disadvantages that may occur as a result of being a member of a particular ethnic group |
| **Ethnography** | The study of people in their natural environment using qualitative methods, particularly participant observation |
| **Expressive documents** | Diaries, letters, paintings and other secondary data that reveal the personal side of a person's life |
| **Expressive roles** | Parsons argued that women were naturally caring and were therefore suitable for the caring and nurturing roles in families and households |
| **False class consciousness** | A Marxist concept, referring to the acceptance by the working class of their position as normal and natural, a failure to recognize their exploitation and oppression by the bourgeoisie |
| **Feminism** | A number of different theories which explain the position of women in society; a common thread is the view that society is patriarchal and women experience different degrees of inequality |
| **Feminization of the elderly** | The process of the balance between males and females over 60 being skewed in favour of women, as a result of the better life expectancy of women compared to men |
| **Fragmentation** | Breaking up into small pieces; may refer to social classes breaking up or individual identities. Associated with postmodernism |
| **Fuel poverty** | Fuel poverty is when a household has to spend more than 10% of its income on energy |
| **Gatekeeper** | The person or persons who are able to give a researcher access to the people they want to study |
| **Gendered roles** | Traditional male and female roles, e.g. women as carers and men as breadwinners |
| **Gender pay gap** | The difference in pay between males and females; on average, women earn less than men |
| **Genderquake** | Used by Naomi Wolf to describe the changing relationships between men and women and the shift of power towards women |
| **Generalization** | The ability to apply the findings of some research to the whole of the population being studied |
| **Globalization** | The process of the world becoming increasingly interconnected socially, economically and culturally |
| **Go native** | This occurs when a researcher becomes so involved with the group being studied that he or she loses sight of their role as a researcher; associated with ethnographic research |
| **Grey power** | The influence of the elderly, often linked to their financial power but also used in relation to their social and political influence |
| **Hawthorne effect** | When those being studied behave differently as a result of knowing that they are being researched |
| **Hegemonic masculinity** | Characterized by a dominant male who has a traditional view of men as patriarchal and who believes men should be the breadwinner |

| Hegemony | A concept initially used by the Marxist theorist Gramsci to mean the dominance of the intellectual and cultural ideas of a social class, usually the ruling class |
|---|---|
| Hierarchical relationship | Used by feminist researchers to describe the nature of the traditional interviewer/interviewee relationship |
| Horizontal segregation | This is the extent to which men and women are employed in different occupational groups; women are largely found in the five 'c's, caring, cashiering, catering, cleaning and clerical |
| Hybridity | The development of cultures based on the combination of aspects of a range of cultures including music, food and clothes |
| Hypothesis | A statement of what the research will test |
| Ideological state apparatus | Institutions such as education, religion or the media, which are part of the superstructure and which transmit the ideas of the ruling class and persuade other social classes to agree with them |
| Ideology | A set of beliefs based on the ideas of the ruling classes |
| Ideology of romance | The view of love and romance as portrayed in the media, rather than being based on the realities of most people's life experiences |
| Income | Monies earned as a result of employment, pensions and savings and investments |
| Infrastructure | A term used by Marxists to describe the economic base of a society |
| Insider status | Belonging to a group; having access to the group's secrets or knowledge |
| Institutional racism | The failure of organizations to provide appropriate policies and practices to people because of their colour, culture or ethnic origin; the rules and regulations of organizations having built-in racist assumptions |
| Instrumental roles | Parsons argued that men were most suited to the role of breadwinner |
| Interpretivism | A number of theories come under this heading, but all are based on the view that individuals and social groups can construct the social world. Interpretivists are interested in the meanings people attach to their own actions and the actions of others |
| Interviewer effect | The ways in which the social characteristics of an interviewer may affect the responses of the interviewee |
| Ladettes | Girls who behave in a similar way to lads; drinking, swearing and generally behaving in a loud and crude manner |
| Laddish | Boyish behaviour, sometimes used when portrayed by females |
| Laddism | The behaviour by young males involving binge drinking, swearing and sexism |
| Leaky pipeline | Refers to the gradual loss of women in higher levels of an occupational area |
| Life chances | The extent to which individuals and households are able to access resources seen as desirable, e.g. good health care and education, decent housing and a good job |
| Life expectancy | The average age a person born in a certain year could expect to live to |
| Lumpenproletariat | A Marxist term used to describe those below the proletariat |
| Manipulation | The process of encouraging children to behave according to their gender, e.g. boys expected to be brave and not cry for too long when they fall or are hurt |

| | |
|---|---|
| **March of progress** | The theory that the position of children and families is gradually improving |
| **Marginalization** | The process of being excluded from mainstream society, experienced by those on the edge of society who lack power |
| **Mask of ageing** | The postmodern view of ageing, which is that at any age people can act or seem similar to those of other age groups. It is particularly associated with older people who are bombarded by the media to persuade them to try to remain young-looking |
| **Material deprivation** | Not having those things that most people are able to have, e.g. decent housing and a healthy diet |
| **Material resources** | The goods that make life acceptable for most people, e.g. clothing, food and housing |
| **Methodological pluralism** | An approach that is usually in two stages, the methods used being of equal status; a strategy often used by realists who want to study different aspects of the research question |
| **Mixed methods** | Using a combination of methods |
| **Mode of production** | A Marxist concept to describe the economic basis of society and the relationships that are a part of that |
| **Morbidity** | The rate of illness and disease in a population or social group |
| **Mortality** | The number of people per 100 000 of the population who die within a given period; it is important to note that it is sometimes expressed as 'per 1 000 of the population' |
| **Narrative** | A form of life history interview which allows the person or sometimes a group to tell the story or stories of their lives |
| **New man** | A man who is sensitive, caring, willing to share his feelings and also willing to do a share of the household tasks and childcare, argued by some as being simply a media creation |
| **Norms** | A generally agreed way of behaving based on shared values, e.g. not lying when honesty is a shared value |
| **Objectivity** | A scientific approach to the study of society free from the bias and values of the researchers |
| **Observation** | Studying people and groups in their natural environments; primarily used by interpretivists but observation matrixes are occasionally used by positivists |
| **Old-boy network** | The informal links between males who went to the same public schools and who in adulthood provide each other with contacts, jobs and other favours. There is increasing evidence of an 'old girl network' being used by top business women |
| **Operationalize** | To measure abstract concepts by defining them in research, for example by writing questionnaire questions |
| **Oppression** | A Marxist concept used to explain how the working class are controlled by those with power |
| **Overt observation** | When those being observed are aware of the researcher's presence |
| **Participant observation** | When a researcher blends into the life of those being researched, e.g. working on a building site to observe how construction workers behave |
| **Patriarchy** | A society, such as the contemporary UK, which is male dominated |

| | |
|---|---|
| **Patterns** | A consistent relationship between two or more variables, e.g. sociologists try to explain the patterns of educational achievement in relation to social class, ethnicity and gender |
| **Pilot study** | A test run of a study to check for potential problems |
| **Polarization** | The process of opposites developing, e.g. between the rich and the poor |
| **Positivism** | A theory which suggests that the social world can be studied using the methods of the natural sciences; the behaviour of individuals and groups can be objectively measured |
| **Post-Fordism** | A move away from mass production to a more flexible way of working and the production of specialized goods |
| **Poverty** | There are two main types: absolute poverty – when people do not have the basic necessities such as food, shelter, clothing and water; relative poverty – when people are unable to have the things that are seen as being desirable, which the majority of society has access to |
| **Power** | The ability of an individual or group to persuade others to do what they want even if the individual or group do not want to do it |
| **Proletarianization** | The de-skilling of white-collar jobs |
| **Proletariat** | A Marxist term for those who own only their labour power; the working class |
| **Qualitative data** | Data that can be expressed in the form of words |
| **Quantitative data** | Data that can be expressed numerically |
| **Race** | A biological construct, which states that people can be characterized on the basis of their biological characteristics such as skin colour |
| **Race discrimination** | Treating one racial group less favourably than others |
| **Racialized class fractions** | The view that in any class minority ethnic groups will be of a lower status within the class compared to the dominant white group |
| **Racism** | Discriminatory behaviour on the basis of a person's biological characteristics |
| **Random sampling** | A sampling technique which gives everyone the same chance of being picked |
| **Rapport** | Development of a relationship between the interviewer and the interviewee |
| **Reflexivity** | The willingness of the researcher to consider the implications of the methods they are using; the extent to which their values are affecting the research and what implications the research might be having on those being researched – a strategy used by feminists |
| **Reliability** | The extent to which the research could be repeated and the same or similar results obtained |
| **Representativeness/ representative** | The extent to which a sample is a fair reflection of the target population |
| **Reproduction of the class system** | The way(s) in which the class system is reproduced, e.g. by the education system |

| | |
|---|---|
| **Researcher imposition** | The way(s) in which a researcher may impose his or her own values on the research process; often used in relation to interpretivists and the analysis of data but can also be applied to positivists at the point of devising a questionnaire or interview schedule |
| **Reserve army of labour** | The idea that there are groups with little power who can be hired when the demand for labour goes up and then fired when it goes down; usually applied to women and minority ethnic groups |
| **Respondent validation** | Most commonly used by interpretivists who ask those they are researching to look at their findings and give feedback on them in terms of whether they have accurately portrayed the lives of the respondents |
| **Sampling frame** | A list of the survey or target population, e.g. a school register |
| **Semiology** | The study of signs and symbols in order to decode and understand the messages contained in the text |
| **Semi-structured interviews** | Interviews that combine elements of structured interviews and unstructured interviews |
| **Sex** | Biological differences between males and females |
| **Sex discrimination** | The unfavourable treatment of one sex compared to the other, specifically because of their sex |
| **Sex roles** | The different ways in which men and women are supposed to behave, e.g. women as carers and men as breadwinners |
| **Shared values** | The values that most people in society agree to, e.g. honesty |
| **Sift and sort** | A concept used by Davis and Moore to describe the way(s) in which people are allocated roles in society via examinations and other competitive means |
| **Social capital** | The people that a person or family knows, who can help in some way; usually used with reference to the middle and upper classes who may know people with some influence who can help them achieve what they want to achieve or gain access to those who will help them to achieve |
| **Social class** | A system of stratification; Marxists use class in preference to stratification, as it highlights the relationship between the different strata in society |
| **Social closure** | The exclusion of people from a social group, e.g. by examination or social connections |
| **Social cohesion** | The idea that everyone is valued and there are common values and beliefs that bind people together |
| **Social construction** | The view that the social world is made by social processes, e.g. interpretivists argue that questionnaires are socially constructed by the researchers designing them and they also argue that crime statistics are a result of the decisions made by the police about what to record |
| **Social differences** | The similarity or dissimilarity to others, e.g. gender, class, ethnicity and age |
| **Social exclusion** | A term used by the Labour governments under Blair to describe those who are too poor to participate in mainstream society |

| Social facts | A concept used by Durkheim to describe values, institutions and beliefs, which may or may not be able to be observed and measured, but do exist over and above individual consciousness |
|---|---|
| Social inequalities | Having advantages or disadvantages compared to other people |
| Socialization | The process of learning to conform to the dominant norms and values in society; the expected patterns of behaviour. The primary agent of socialization is the family and the main secondary agents of socialization are education, the media, religion, peers and work |
| Socially mobile | The extent to which a society is an open one and people can readily move from one class to another |
| Social policy | A set of principles, sometimes laid down in law, which cover areas such as education and health |
| Social solidarity | A Durkheimian concept, concerned with the extent to which people are socially integrated into society and social groups within society, and the ways in which they adhere to the generally agreed norms and values of the group or society |
| Social stratification | The way in which societies are layered with some groups being ranked above or below others |
| Social structure | The way in which society is organized |
| Social survey | A way to collect large amounts of quantitative data in a logical and scientific way, which is considered to be objective |
| Status | A person's social position or standing within society; may be ascribed, e.g. the queen, or achieved, e.g. a doctor |
| Stratified random sampling | A sampling technique which, by dividing the target population into groups which the researcher is interested in studying, attempts to ensure that the sample is a fair reflection of the target population |
| Structural constraints | The way(s) in which individuals are prevented from making free choices, e.g. household income may mean that the household cannot move in order to be in a particular school's catchment area |
| Structural theory | Theories such as functionalism which argue that individuals are shaped by society |
| Structure | The social institutions around which society is organized and which may constrain individuals from exercising agency |
| Structured interviews | Formal interviews based on pre-set questions |
| Subjective | Allowing the views and values of the researcher to be part of the research; interpretive sociologists and feminists argue that research cannot and, for some of them, should not be objective |
| Super class | Adonis and Pollard identified a class of newly rich bankers and professionals who earn very high salaries and are sometimes referred to as 'fat cats' |
| Superstructure | A term used by Marxists to describe the parts of society that are not involved directly in the production of wealth; these include the agencies of socialization |
| Target population | The group that the researcher is interested in studying and from whom a sample may be drawn |

| Trend | A tendency or a direction, usually over time, e.g. there is a trend for more households to have access to the internet |
|---|---|
| Triangulation | The use of more than one method, usually one or more that collects quantitative data and one or more that collects qualitative data |
| Typical | Applied to a sampling unit where it could be described as similar to, or the same as, the majority of the target population |
| Underclass | A contested concept, applied to those below the working class whose poverty often excludes them from participation in mainstream society; they are marginalized |
| Unified working class | The traditional Marxist view that there is one united working class |
| Unstructured interviews | Informal intervals, sometimes referred to as structured conversations, in which the researcher is able to probe the interviewee for additional information and the interviewee can ask for clarification |
| Upper class | A small, very wealthy group comprising the traditional aristocracy, the capitalists who own the means of production and more recently those who have acquired wealth through sporting activities or popular music – see also super class |
| Validity | The extent to which the research is a true picture of the social reality of those being studied |
| Value freedom | The view that sociology and sociological research should be as objective as possible and that the views of the researcher should not influence the research in any way |
| Values | General principles or guidelines on behaviour; the things that members of society hold to be important, e.g. honesty, loyalty and personal achievement |
| *Verstehen* | A term used by Weber meaning gaining an understanding of how those being researched feel, or seeing the world through their eyes; ethnographers aspire to achieve this |
| Vertical segregation | Occupational stratification by gender; compared to men, women tend to be in jobs with low status and low pay, which occurs in specific organizations and the labour market in general |
| Wealth | Material assets in the form of property, which are deemed important by a society, e.g. land, stocks and shares and valuables such as jewellery and paintings; not essential to a person's day-to-day needs |

# Index